Let's Get Real

This new book is a vital resource for any teacher or administrator to help students tackle issues of race, class, gender, religion, and cultural background. Authors Martha Caldwell and Oman Frame, both lifelong educators, offer a series of teaching strategies designed to encourage conversation and personal reflection, enabling students to think creatively, rather than stereotypically, about difference. Using the Transformational Inquiry model, your students will learn to explore their own identities, share stories and thoughts with their peers, learn more through reading and research, and ultimately take personal, collaborative action to bring about social change in their communities.

You'll learn how to:

- facilitate dynamic classroom discussions in a safe and empathetic environment;
- encourage students to think and talk objectively about complex and sensitive issues such as race, gender, and social class;
- help students cultivate valuable communication, critical thinking, and writing skills while developing their identities in a healthy way; and
- develop your teacher identity in a positive way to better support your students' growth and self-discovery.

The strategies in this book can be adapted for any middle school or high school curriculum, and each chapter includes a variety of lesson plans and handouts that you can use in the classroom immediately. These resources can also be downloaded from the authors' website: www.ichangecollaborative.com.

Martha Caldwell and **Oman Frame** are cofounders of iChange Collaborative Consulting, where they train teachers, administrators, and students in diversity education, global competency, and social emotional learning. They also teach integrated middle school humanities curricula at the Paideia School in Atlanta, Georgia.

Other Eye On Education Books
Available from Routledge
(www.routledge.com/eyeoneducation)

The Classes They Remember:
Using Role Plays to Bring Social Studies and English to Life
David Sherrin

Judging for Themselves:
Using Mock Trials to Bring Social Studies and English to Life
David Sherrin

History Class Revisited:
Tools and Projects to Engage Middle School Students
in Social Studies
Jody Passanisi

7 Ways to Transform the Lives of Wounded Students
Joe Hendershott

Mentoring Is a Verb:
Strategies for Improving College and Career Readiness
Russ Olwell

Educating Students in Poverty:
Effective Practices for Leadership and Teaching
Mark Lineburg and Rex Gearheart

Teaching Practices from America's Best Urban Schools:
A Guide for School and Classroom Leaders
Joseph Johnson, Cynthia Uline, and Lynne Perez

Let's Get Real

Exploring Race, Class, and Gender Identities in the Classroom

Martha Caldwell and Oman Frame

Routledge
Taylor & Francis Group

NEW YORK AND LONDON

First published 2017
by Routledge
711 Third Avenue, New York, NY 10017

and by Routledge
2 Park Square, Milton Park, Abingdon, Oxon, OX14 4RN

Routledge is an imprint of the Taylor & Francis Group, an informa business

Library of Congress Cataloging in Publication Data
A catalog record for this book has been requested

ISBN: 978-1-138-68522-2 (hbk)
ISBN: 978-1-138-68523-9 (pbk)
ISBN: 978-1-315-54337-6 (ebk)

Typeset in Palatino and Myriad Pro
by Florence Production Ltd, Stoodleigh, Devon, UK

Printed and bound in the United States of America by Publishers Graphics,
LLC on sustainably sourced paper.

Contents

Additional Resources

The lesson plans in this book, along with additional materials, are available on Martha and Oman's website at www.ichangecollaborative.com. You will also find the "Teacher Identity Group Study Guide," a resource for teachers who would like to explore their own identities in professional learning communities or read and discuss the book with colleagues.

Click on the Teacher Resources page to download materials.

Meet the Authors

Martha Caldwell and **Oman Frame** teach at the Paideia School in Atlanta, Georgia. In addition, they consult with schools, present workshops for students, and offer a summer teaching institute for social justice educators. Articles about their work have appeared in *Schoolbook, Middle School Journal, Independent Schools Magazine*, and *Youth Today*. They can be reached through their website at www.ichangecollaborative.com.

Martha has taught for over twenty years. She has designed curricula in Mexican History and Culture, African American History, Peace and Conflict in the Middle East, Response to Climate Change, Archetypes in Fairy Tales, Contemplating God, Poetry and Activism, Film of the Civil Rights Era, Blogging about Books, Dragons Lore, History of English, and Rites of Passage. She sponsors the Girls Mentoring program and the Gay Straight Alliance. She has four children and three grandchildren.

Oman has twenty years of experience in teaching and diversity leadership. He is the Middle-Level Director of Equity and Justice at Paideia. Oman's story was featured in Ned Hollowell's *Positively ADD: Real Success Stories to Inspire Your Dreams*. His innovative teaching was featured on ION TV's *Everyday Heroes*, and he was named an 11 Alive News Teacher of the Week. *Ebony Magazine* listed his crew as the "Coolest Black Family in America." He and his wife, Naimah, have two daughters.

Acknowledgments

Many people have contributed to this book, and we are grateful to them all. Special recognition goes to those who came before us and struggled for equity and justice. We acknowledge that we stand on the shoulders of great teachers, thinkers, and activists, and we hope this book makes a small contribution to a larger body of work. We acknowledge the Paideia School, principally Paul Bianchi, for supporting teachers and giving us a place to develop our passions. Our colleagues here inspire us daily. Special thanks goes to the junior high team, especially Jennifer Swift, Tom Painting, Rachel Gomez Peterson, Sydney Cleland, and Andy Sarvady, for supporting and reflecting this work in their classes and beyond. Greg Changnon, in particular, has been a source of encouragement and a good friend. The legacy of Martha and Bernie Schein is everywhere in this book. We would like to thank our editor, Lauren, for her enthusiasm about the book and the team at Routledge for guiding us through this process. Thanks also to Eddy Hernandez, Natalie Bernstein, José Cordero, Philip McAdoo, Keith White, Danielle Stewart, and the teachers who have participated in our institutes. And, most of all, we thank our students.

Martha's Acknowledgments

A shout out to my family for their unwavering love and support. Wes and Christy, Julia and José, Lee, and Joanna inspire me with their very lives. Julia and Lee read early versions of this work and took me to task. My grandchildren and joy machines, Javi, Ian, and Joaquin, reminded me to play and kept me smiling. My sister Carole's constant love throughout my life and especially during this project kept me saner than I otherwise would have been. I am also richly blessed with the finest friends a human being could ever hope for. Elana has been a consistent source of support. Shasta sustained me with laugher and guided me with love. Randy has been true blue. Vanessa has been there throughout. And Nathan believed in me all the way to the finish line. I am so deeply grateful for you all.

Oman's Acknowledgments

I would like to acknowledge the unwavering support of my life partner, my wisdom, my earth, Naimah Oladuwa-Frame. Her steadfast and dynamic support has and will always help me in the pursuit of equity and justice. She has held me to a high standard, as well as loved me infinitely through this process. I would also like to thank and share this with my children, Suriyah and Uchenna. Your presence in my life is one of purpose, love, and creativity. I embrace the lessons you teach me each day, as well as the joy you provide. Thank you for choosing me. The vein of family runs to the core as well. I couldn't have done it without the guidance and love of Leo, Janice, Kairi, Stephanie, Jackson, Omowale, Geri, Onaje, Kemit, Rasamen, Tyrone, Amanda, and Nyla, Team Darden, Andre Vega, Howard "Spook" Johnson, and Andre Robert-Lee.

Preface

We are teachers who work in classrooms with kids every day. Our Transformational Inquiry (TI) method did not begin with theory but emerged from our daily practice. In fact, we stumbled upon our integrated social studies and language arts curriculum quite by accident. We were designing a course on climate change and wanted our students to connect the issues of climate change to social justice. We wanted them to recognize that climate change will impact the economically disadvantaged more severely than the economically secure. We wanted them to realize that climate change is about more than just recycling and being green. We wanted them to see that masses of people on the planet could be displaced, the poorest regions of the world could face food shortages, and the people least equipped to survive could be the victims of famine and disease. We wanted them to see the larger systems that play a role in creating social inequity. Ultimately, we hoped we could inspire them to assume ownership of changing the world and making it a better place. So in order to offer them a background for understanding systemic injustice, we designated the first two-week unit to address topics related to their own identities: race, class, and gender.

That two-week unit on social identity expanded to fill the entire semester, and it ultimately became the social studies/language arts course we teach every year. Why? Because our students were inspired. They were excited to have a forum to share their experiences. They were making important connections: learning how they were different, how they were the same, and how systems of power in the wider world reflected their identities back to them.

When our students began exploring their social identities, we knew immediately we had tapped into a wellspring of motivation. They were engaged, inspired, and achieving, and we saw the effects in their thinking and writing. They were clearly motivated by what they were learning and began talking about it to their friends. Their parents told us they were talking about it at home. Other teachers began adapting our method for their classes. We were excited, and we wanted to share what we were learning. We began making conference presentations and conducting workshops for faculties and students in other schools.

Over successive years, we've expanded what works, streamlined our approach, tried a host of new activities and exercises, and integrated the original social studies course with literature, writing, and grammar. We now refer to our specific methodology as Transformational Inquiry (TI). We teach the TI method to elementary through secondary level teachers in an annual institute each summer. Teachers are using aspects of our template in middle and high school advisory groups, English, history, ethics, biology, math, and civics classes, as well as in middle school social studies and language arts. Athletic coaches use it in their sports programs for team building.

Our Background

People frequently ask us how we came to this work, and it is important for teachers who work with identity issues to disclose their social locations. By way of introduction, Martha is white and Oman is black. Both have taught in urban public schools with predominantly low income and students of color populations. We both currently teach at the Paideia School in Atlanta, an independent school where the nonwhite population hovers at around 30 percent and 25 percent of students receive financial aid. Paideia offers teachers remarkable authority over their classrooms, encouraging them to develop innovative curriculum based on their passions. We have received tremendous support from colleagues, administrators, parents, and students in developing this method.

Oman grew up in the predominantly black area of Southwest Atlanta. In school, he struggled with dyslexia and attention issues. When his family moved to Massachusetts, he was one of only a few people of color in his high school. Like many students of color in majority white settings, he learned quickly and painfully to code switch, revealing only a small part of his identity at school. His learning issues combined with his marginalized racial identity resulted in feelings of inadequacy and low self-esteem. Like many young people, he internalized the stereotypes projected onto him and struggled with academic performance. After a year in a majority white college, he transferred to Hampton University, a historically black college, where he thrived, coming to understand the multidimensional experiences of black Americans in a historical and global context. He realized that much of his struggle in school was the result of institutional racism, despite the school's good intentions. By learning to identify the negative influences on his young psyche as existing "outside himself," he gained confidence as a learner and began to excel as a student. At Hampton, his sexist conditioning was also challenged. When professors questioned his commitment to ending racism without looking at how he was a part of sexism, he became a strong ally for women's justice. Through the work of feminists such as Patricia Hill Collins and bell hooks, he came to understand the intersecting oppressions of race, gender, and class.

Martha, on the other hand, came of age in the South during the era of segregation. She did not know any people of color until her sixth grade class was forcibly integrated, and she encountered African American students who contradicted every stereotype she had been conditioned to believe. In high school, she struggled with attention issues and boredom, dropping out after eleventh grade when she became a mother. Over the next eleven years, she attended college sporadically, mostly at night, while living below the poverty line, struggling to support her children and get an education. During this time, she became active in antiracist and antisexist community groups, exploring the effects of marginalized identities. After graduation, in an effort to finance her children's education, she worked in corporate sales and finance. Unfulfilled, she changed careers in her mid-thirties and began teaching. She entered the classroom at midyear during Act 2, Scene 3 of Macbeth. Most of her students were black, poor, and low achieving. Inspired by the integrity of their stories and recognizing the enormous untapped potential of their intelligence, she enrolled in graduate school where, for the first time in her life, she was excited about learning.

We share our stories because our personal struggles to overcome our own oppression, both internal and institutional, inform our work. We use our identities and histories to steer the study we engage in with students. Oman has a deep understanding of the effects of racism on people of color from personal experience. Martha understands the detrimental, though largely unrecognized, effects of racism on white people and has a grasp of how racism can be successfully challenged. In terms of gender, Martha knows from personal experience how male privilege affects women and girls both psychologically and materially, and in terms of social class, she understands how financial hardships can affect academic performance.

During the evolution of this course, we made an agreement: to work through any issues that arose in our teaching relationship in terms of power and privilege as a result of our own identities. As teachers, we have a lot in common and agree on a great many things. We share a common purpose in that we believe in the inherent intelligence of every student, and we are both committed advocates for equity and justice. Yet we come from vastly different backgrounds. We capitalize on our differences to gain strength as a team, but our differences are not always easy to negotiate. There have been times when we have confronted each other both about our work with students and about issues in our relationship. Oman has confronted Martha about racial insensitivity and, likewise, Martha has challenged Oman when his attitudes betray unconscious gender bias. Yet, because we teach students how to negotiate relationships across differences, we have to work through our differences so we can model what we teach. The secret of our success is that we are committed allies. We recognize that conflict is a part of our relationship, and though these conversations can be difficult, we also see how productive conflict can be. We gain understanding not only of each other's experience, but also of the effects social oppression can have on personal relationships. It isn't always pretty, but every time we experience conflict, we emerge as stronger allies, closer friends, and better teachers.

Building a network of allies is imperative in challenging oppression. It is important for all teachers, especially those who are committed to social justice teaching, diversity and inclusion practices, and critical pedagogy, to develop a support network. The nature of oppressive conditioning is that it alienates us from others; but it also alienates us from ourselves. By its very nature, teaching can be an isolating profession. All too often we go into the separate worlds of our classrooms, cut off from the support and nurturance of other adults. As a result, teachers are often hungry for connections. Sharing stories with other teachers is highly invigorating, and forging relationships is crucial to sustaining our work. Teachers in our institutes tell us the close connections they make with each other are a source of strength. For several years, teachers have maintained their connections through an Internet forum and continue to share experiences and resources with each other.

We stress the need to consciously and deliberately develop a network of supportive relationships with like-minded teachers to overcome the isolation inherent in the present structure of the teaching profession and in the present structure of personal identity. Race, gender, and class insensitivity, whether conscious or unconscious, intentional or unintentional, is not uncommon even in the most progressive of environments. We invite you to explore your identity in a group with other teachers as you read this book. We still live in a world struggling to overcome our personal and collective histories. We need to know we are not alone.

How to Use This Book

This book is for teachers who want to change the face of education. They hear the imperative call to teach students to think critically, and they recognize that empathy is a key ingredient of higher order learning. They want to strengthen their theoretical foundation and position their teaching in practical methods to answer this call. They understand learning as an exhilarating, generative experience and want to engage their students in a dynamic process to create synergistic learning communities. They want to inspire their students to engage in learning more deeply, and they know they can accomplish this through curricula that addresses their students' developmental needs, personal interests, and emerging identities. They are genuinely interested in their students and want to assist them in reaching their full potential as human beings.

Education at its best is a transformative process. Integrating the personal, social, cognitive, and action dimensions of learning results in positive personal and social change. The primary goal of the TI method is to facilitate healthy identity development in the context of a diverse learning community. An identity-safe classroom encourages empathy, positive peer acceptance, and the inclusion of diverse ideas. In such environments, individuality and diversity flourish simultaneously.

Healthy identity development is not just an inside job. For a healthy identity to emerge, young people need to have their identities validated and supported. They need to see their finest qualities and human aspirations mirrored by teachers and peers alike. Because students want nothing more than to be accepted in a community, they eagerly acquire the TI communication skill set, and the result is that their budding identities are allowed a place to emerge.

The emergence of a healthy identity results in a cascade of positive outcomes. Students learn valuable communication skills: respectful listening, authentic sharing, how to give supportive feedback, and the value of empathy. As they mirror each other's experiences, they form deeper connections with each other. Attention to processing feelings allows their innate capacity for critical reasoning to emerge. As their identities become stronger, they develop the voice to speak out on their own behalf and on the behalf of others. As they come to understand their capacity to effect change in the world, they find meaning and purpose in their lives. Along the way, they develop a host of academic skills: critical reading, analysis, inquiry-based research, and writing. Perhaps most importantly, they learn to love learning. Through the interplay of information from the personal, social, cognitive, and action domains, a synthesis is created that lays the groundwork for higher order thinking.

The TI method provides a template that teachers can infuse with their own passions and expertise. Because the method is versatile and can be adapted to any curriculum, teachers are using aspects of the TI template in a variety of settings and at every grade level. Teachers of young children facilitate dynamic conversations about their identity-related experiences using picture books. Diversity directors use the interpersonal exercises to stimulate dialogue during "seminar days" devoted to school-wide education about race, class, and gender.

We encourage teachers to adapt these lessons to fit their students' needs and to complement their existing curriculum. José, a first grade teacher, for instance, begins the year by having his students generate rules for respect. "The kids always want an inclusive classroom, and this activity sets that up," José says. "The rules help make the meaning of empathy explicit, but empathy is more powerful than rules. If we're focusing on rules, we're not paying attention to how people feel and the real consequences of their behavior." He uses daily class meetings to discuss social dynamics and teach relationship skills.

Miguel, a fith grade teacher, asks his students to choose current events articles to share in class, and the articles they choose often reflect their social identities. Last year, several African American students brought in articles about police shootings. Hispanic students brought in articles about immigration. Without presenting any one viewpoint as "correct," Miguel asks his students to share their feelings and opinions about such controversial topics. He finds his ten-year-old students can respect each other's perspectives and gain valuable insight about their differences, as well as their similarities, through these discussions. Miguel's students are not too young to understand that life experiences influence perspective, an important step toward critical thinking.

Jasmin, a seventh grade teacher, has her students share their experience with bullying in "Fish Bowls." In literature class, her students form circles to interpret Tupac Shakur's poem "The Rose that Grew from Concrete," and discuss the question "Are people controlled by their environments, or can they control their environments?" Jasmin draws parallels from these discussions when they study the Holocaust, and eventually to their research on ethnic and social identity groups impacted by World War II.

Greg's middle school students explore their identities in a drama workshop. They discuss challenging aspects of their identities and use their personal experiences to create backstories for the characters they will portray. This exercise helps them infuse their acting with authentic passion. To further prepare, they read coming-of-age stories with identity-based themes and study method acting.

Caroline's high school math students begin the year with an inquiry into learning. They discuss their emotional relationship to learning in general and to learning math specifically. She introduces the concepts of cognitive dissonance, learning edge, and essential questions. She introduces the idea of stereotype threat, and her students discuss the role of race and gender identity in the math achievement gap.

Many of the student stories and comments in the book come from our classroom, but others come from students and teachers we have met through our work in other schools. The names and identifying circumstances of stories have been changed, though their quotes are taken verbatim from their reflective writing and self-evaluations. Their comments reveal common themes: their relationships are strengthened; they are motivated to learn; their capacity for thinking is expanded; they feel more empathy and understanding for others; and they feel more confidence as learners and teachers.

Layout of the Book

All TI lessons reflect the Common Core State Standards (CCSS) in that they align with the main objective: facilitating higher order thinking. In the context of identity explorations, the lessons teach proficiency in reading; identifying main ideas; summarizing, interpreting, and analyzing meaning in texts; identifying bias; synthesizing information from multiple sources; and identifying character motivation. They relate to the CCSS Language Arts standards for instruction to facilitate speaking and listening skills and link to many states' standards for social emotional learning.

Because teachers must provide an educational basis for their practice, especially when using innovative methods, the pedagogical foundations for TI are outlined in the first three chapters. The method is contextualized in existing educational traditions and the research that supports it. The next four chapters detail the curricular units: Inquiry Into Identity, Inquiry Into Race, Inquiry Into Gender, and Inquiry Into Social Class. Each of these chapters introduces key concepts related to identity inquiry and describes how to scaffold instruction. Each chapter suggests materials and provides sample lesson plans. The final chapter, Teacher Identity Work, analyzes teacher identity in a problematic profession and calls for teachers to take action for change.

Chapter 1, Teaching and Learning by Discovery, lays the foundation for identity exploration in the classroom. It introduces the four domains of learning in TI—personal, social, cognitive, and action—and explains their interrelationship in the knowledge-building process. It discusses the meaning of learning and defines knowledge construction as both a personal and social/political process. A skeletal structure of inquiries into race, gender, and class is introduced, using examples from our "Inquiry into Identity" curriculum to elucidate how lessons are scaffolded, building on concepts students obtain in personal reflection, social interaction, academic skill building, and active agency.

Chapter 2, Transformational Inquiry: Foundations for Practice, delves more deeply into theory and research from diverse sources and substantiates the TI method, grounding it in existing traditions within the field of education. Chapter 2 describes the relationship between learning and identity, emphasizing the critical window of opportunity for identity formation during adolescence. It outlines the four domains of learning in greater detail, and then describes their effects in the context of identity formation. Finally, it discusses the importance of providing supportive environments for identity exploration in classrooms and schools.

Chapter 3, The Teacher's Role: Facilitating Dynamic Dialogues, explains the underlying philosophy of TI teaching. It discusses the teacher's role in facilitating identity-safe conversations in the classroom, emphasizing the importance of listening, allowing emotional expression, and offering supportive feedback that validates students' identities. Chapter 3 outlines seven principles that support facilitation of sensitive conversations about identity. It emphasizes the importance of student feedback and communication guidelines that foster healthy interactions between students and teachers and among students.

Chapter 4, Inquiry Into Identity: Introductory Explorations, provides a template through which students begin to explore their personal and social identities. It describes how to establish identity safety in the classroom and discusses the intersection of social identity with learning identity. It includes a set of activities that prepare students to engage in conversations about race, gender, and social class identities in greater depth in subsequent units, but these lessons have also been used as a stand-alone unit in student advisory groups, seminar days focused on race and gender identity, and as adjunct curriculum in high school classrooms to explore identity-based learning. Chapter 4 explains how to scaffold concepts and provides four sample lesson plans.

Chapter 5, Inquiry Into Race, emphasizes the importance of strengthening racial identities in schools, as well as the importance of examining United States' history through a racial lens. It highlights the need for teachers to develop race consciousness by comparing it with a color-blind mindset. It describes race as a master category of oppression and discusses student responses in conversations about race. The second section of Chapter 5 outlines the curriculum's conceptual framework, scaffolding concepts that introduce students to racial issues through the four domains of learning. Each concept references lesson plans, and four sample lesson plans are included.

Chapter 6, Inquiry Into Gender, addresses the importance of gender studies in schools, particularly during adolescence, as a response to bullying and relational aggression. It contains a brief description of gender identity formation and illustrates the effects of gender identity explorations using student stories. The second section of Chapter 6 demonstrates how important concepts are scaffolded through the personal, social, cognitive, and action domains, describing specific lessons in the curriculum. Four sample lesson plans are included.

Chapter 7, Inquiry Into Social Class, explores the effects of social class identity on learning and in schools, emphasizing the relationship between socioeconomic status and school achievement. It stresses the importance of positive class identities and demonstrates the effect of inquiries into social class using student stories. The second part of the chapter outlines key concepts and describes specific lessons, using stories from the classroom as examples. Four sample lesson plans are included.

Chapter 8, Teacher Identity Work, concerns the effects of social identities on teachers, including and emphasizing the importance of a strong teaching identity. Teachers need strong identities themselves in order to guide students in identity exploration; however, in a profession that requires a high degree of caring, yet carries low authority and little social esteem, teacher identity itself can be problematic. Chapter 8 explores the effects of the current educational climate on teacher identity formation. It examines the historical effects of white female identity in the teaching profession and describes issues that teachers of color encounter in schools. It calls for greater teacher authority in the classroom and re-envisions schools as places that advance social empowerment.

We hope groups of teachers will read this book together and use the activities in the Teacher Identity Group Study Guide to explore their own identities in professional learning communities. The effects of racism, sexism, classism, and a host of other "isms," permeate our society, as well as our individual and collective consciousness. Whether we are black, white, male, female, or other, it would be naïve to think that we, as individuals and members of identity groups ourselves, have not been affected by the institutionalized nature of oppression. No one is immune, as it operates in all our lives. Neglecting to recognize and address our own discomfort, determine its source, and process the surrounding feelings can result in a "failure of empathy" for our students. In addition, these activities can provide meaningful facilitation experience, as Teacher Identity Groups simulate the classroom experience of students in important ways. A support network of like-minded teachers is an invaluable component to continuing professional growth and development, especially for those committed to social justice.

More lesson plans for each of the four curricular units (Inquiry Into Identity, Inquiry Into Race, Inquiry Into Gender, and Inquiry Into Social Class), as well as the Teacher Identity Group Study Guide, can be downloaded from the iChange Collaborative Teacher Resources page at www.ichangecollaborative. com/ichange/Teacher_Resources.html.

1

Teaching and Learning
by Discovery

Karla, an African American student, told the class about the time a white friend invited her home to play after school. As they climbed into the back of the minivan, her friend's mother tried to buckle Karla's seatbelt for her. Karla pushed her hand away, saying she could do it herself. The mother stepped back, looked surprised, and called Karla a painful racial slur. As Karla told the story, her eyes filled with tears. Even though the incident happened five years earlier, the pain was still fresh. At the time it happened, she felt ashamed and didn't even tell her parents.

Her classmates responded to her story with indignation. Maggie, a white student, was outraged. "How dare she? You were only a child!" she cried. Seeing Karla tear up again, Maggie moved across the room and put her arms around her. "You are not the one who should feel ashamed, Karla. That woman should be ashamed!" Other students echoed Maggie's response.

It took courage for Karla to share her story, and Maggie's and her other classmates' strong support helped her move beyond the shame she had internalized. But the conversation wasn't just important for Karla and other students of color who had experienced racism. For those who had never experienced it, empathy for Karla made the pain of racism suddenly very real. Many white students had known Karla for years, and like Maggie, they considered her their friend. Yet they had no idea she had experienced such blatant racism. Hearing Karla's story, they felt compassion and respect. They felt honored to be trusted, and like Maggie, they felt protective.

In "Inquiry into Identity: Race, Class and Gender (RCG)," our students' stories serve as springboards for higher order learning. Through sharing personal experiences and listening to each other respectfully, they form a learning community in which examined thinking emerges. They gain important insights about their own identities, while learning about the lives of their classmates. They make important interpersonal connections, which allow them to form alliances across divisions and think creatively, rather than stereotypically, about differences. When their experience is the subject of shared reflection, learning becomes relevant and engagement increases (Baxter Magolda, 1999; Duncan-Andrade & Morrell, 2008; Friere, 1970; Shor, 1992; Wink, 2005).

Our students live and breathe the politics of social justice every day in their lives both at home and at school. They understand the effects of social power in the hallways; they know the subtle workings of the social hierarchies during lunch and in their social media networks. This knowledge can be used to bridge understanding of how systems of power function in the wider world. Through inquiries into literature, histories, politics, and cultures, they connect what they know from personal experience to how power and privilege function in institutions like schools, religions, governments, and businesses (Caldwell, 2012). By forging a connection between their academic and personal worlds, students bring their personal lives to school and take their schoolwork home to be discussed over dinner.

> Our students live and breathe the politics of social justice every day in their lives both at home and at school.

The Transformational Inquiry Method

All learning is channeled through the identities our students claim. Transformational Inquiry (TI) guides students on an identity quest by scaffolding instruction through four domains of learning: personal, social, cognitive, and action. The personal domain involves interpersonal self-reflection. Students learn to attend to, regulate, and process feelings, recognizing their rich inner landscape as a source of learning. The social domain involves sharing experiences, listening respectfully to others, and giving supportive feedback. Through a series of activities, students develop communication skills that facilitate empathy and build an identity-safe learning community. In the cognitive domain, students acquire academic content and practice collaboration, research, and presentation skills. Studies in histories, politics, literature, and other academic disciplines consolidate insights gained in the personal and social domains to expand their worldviews. In the action domain, they put what they learn into practice, not only in their daily interactions, but also through participatory action projects they design. Research shows that integrating these domains results in sustained learning (Pelligrino & Hilton, 2012). Self-exploration strengthens identity, improves self-esteem, and accelerates academic performance (Cabrera, Milem & Marx, 2012; Harper & Tuckman, 2006; Romero, Arce & Cammarota, 2009; Steele & Cohn-Vargas, 2013; Toomey & Umana-Taylor, 2012; Valenzuela, 1999).

While the TI process is not linear and learning does not progress in an orderly fashion from one domain to the next, we generally scaffold instruction that begins in the personal realm and moves through the social, cognitive, and action realms accordingly. Of course, students achieve cognitive insights in the personal realm and frequently act on what they learn in the social realm. Academic learning is infused with passion generated in the personal and social realms and integrated by action. Action, likewise, is inspired by personal insight, compassion for others, and cognitive analysis.

TI capitalizes on key developmental needs. Identity formation is the task of adolescence, and the most important work our students will do. They are already questioning who they are and who they want to become, so moving their life experience to the center of the curriculum has profound effects on learning. Gaining awareness of identity-based power and politics gives them the opportunity to develop cognitive resistance and counteract stereotypes they have internalized. As a result, they obtain greater agency during a critical window of identity formation.

According to Richardson, Sinclair, Poteat, and Koenig (2012), over a third of bullying is bias related. Students are frequently targeted because of their social identities: race, gender, religion, perceived sexual orientation, or physical or mental disability. The effects of bullying include: high-risk behaviors, poor grades, and emotional distress, and when bullying is related to core components of a student's identity, the effects are even worse. Having discussions about aspects of identity, such as race, gender, religion, and abilities, can address relational aggression and mitigate its effects. As a result of supportive peer relationships, students are better able to learn and are more engaged with each other in the academic realm (Roseberry, McIntyre & Gonzalez, 2001; Steele & Cohn-Vargas, 2013). Harper and Tuckman (2006) relate positive outcomes, especially among minority students, to positive racial experiences. Experiences that validate

> **Having discussions about aspects of identity, such as race, gender, religion, and abilities, can address relational aggression and mitigate its effects.**

a student's sense of racial identity emerge from carefully designed interactions with other students. Other studies show that conversations about social identity increase perspective taking, critical thinking, and transfer to better academic performance (Berrett, 2012; Gurin, Dey, Hurtado & Gurin, 2002). Learning authentic communication skills facilitates positive and supportive relationships. Through listening to their own voices and the voices of others, students' identities are strengthened, and academic confidence increases.

Knowledge as Power

Learning is an emotional, social, cognitive, and active process, which results in the expansion and reorganization of information into new patterns of thought. The pedagogical tradition of inquiry recognizes that learning is sustained when cognition is integrated with its social, emotional, and creative counterparts (Pelligrino & Hilton, 2012). Proponents believe learning is a natural instinct, human motivation is intrinsic, and the thrill of discovery serves as its own reward. In their review of research spanning several decades, Barron and Darling-Hammond (2008) substantiate the effectiveness of inquiry and emphasize the power of collaboration and learning-in-community on social, emotional, and academic development.

Critical inquiry educators believe that the practice of education must be transformed to address the needs of students and designed to help them solve the persistent problems faced in the world. They believe that learning does not consist of the capacity to regurgitate content information fed to them by teachers, but rather, true learning is a journey of discovery that begins with the discovery of self. Their aim is to empower students to think for themselves, to learn what they most need to know, and to act in their own interest. According to Ira Shor (1999), "Critical literacy thus challenges the status quo in an effort to discover alternative paths for self and social development" (para. 2). Critical pedagogy involves less distinction between the roles of teacher and students because students take an active role in teaching each other.

TI builds on the work of Paulo Friere (1970) and other critical educators such as bell hooks (1994), Marcia Baxter Magolda (1999), Joan Wink (2005), and Ernest Morrell (Duncan-Andrade & Morrell, 2008). Like critical inquiry, TI emphasizes the *process* by which learning occurs rather than the acquisition of *content*. Far too many students come to us with the view that learning is a passive activity. Rather than generating their own questions, they expect teachers to deliver content and tell them what is important to know.

They have learned to measure success in school based on grades alone and have no real connection to learning as an intrinsic drive. They repress authentic questions and instead focus on questions they think will be on the test. When we tell them asking questions is more important than knowing the answers, they are initially confused.

Knowledge does not fall from the sky fully formed. People, rather, generate knowledge, and a classroom at its best becomes a shared learning community in which students generate, rather than consume, knowledge. Learning is driven by questions, and knowledge is a social/political/historical construct, always value laden and always imbued with power (Apple, 2004; Sturrock, 1979; Wortham, 2006). According to Clifford and Marinucci (2008, p. 680), knowledge is not fixed and static, but an ever-evolving construct built by a community of learners:

> Genuine inquiries demand that understanding develops in a public space in which each person's abilities, interests, perspectives, and talents help move everyone else's thinking forward. It is a knowledge-building space in which ideas are at the center, and each individual has a commitment to producing the collective, evolving understanding.

TI provides the framework for students to reflect on learning as a political act. By presenting dominant social paradigms concerning race, gender, and class identities as social/historical/hierarchical constructs, the tenets of "knowledge" belying bias and stereotypes are brought into question. When such tenets have been normalized and internalized, students may have difficulty articulating opposition and resisting their influence even when such ideas cause them harm. The TI process presents perspectives to challenge the status quo and encourages strong, positive identities. The process works through self-examination, the inclusion of student voices, introducing students to multiple perspectives, and creating forums for action.

TI evokes generative themes related to identity: race, class, gender, sexuality, religion, cultural background, and learning styles. Generative themes work to bring unexamined ideas into conscious awareness through a depth method of inquiry. Sharing personal stories facilitates empathy and drives questioning. The relationships formed in the process inspire connections in the academic realm. Inspired by care for their classmates, students feed off of each other's learning. When young men of color, for instance, tell stories of being followed by security guards in the mall, the insidious nature of racial profiling is made explicit for white students who have not experienced racial bias. Students can extrapolate what they learn about each other's lives to better understand racial disparities in the justice system. They move on to study the history of prisons, capital punishment, the drug war, and the prison industrial complex.

Carlos, a Mexican American student, described crossing the border in the trunk of a car with his mother and being abandoned by their coyote in the desert. When he shared his fear that his parents could be deported, other students empathized with him, understanding how painful it would be to be separated from their own parents. That November, when President Obama issued an executive order outlining a process by which Carlos's parents could "come out of the shadows" and gain legal status, students were attuned to this important political event because they could relate Carlos's personal story to events occurring in the national forum. They were eager to learn the constitutional underpinnings of an executive order, and the balance of power in the United States government became real to them.

Thus, the content of the curriculum shifts based on emerging student identities, interests, and current events. Yet they learn important academic skills no matter the content: close reading, critical thinking, effective communication, and clear writing. Through critical reflection, they achieve metacognitive awareness, which results in important insights into themselves, the ways they learn, and the society they live in. They form alliances with each other and feel a sense of belonging in the classroom, which counteracts the alienation from school so many students experience. Consequently, they learn more and communicate what they have learned with greater depth and insight. Not only are they learning how to learn; they are learning to love learning.

> **Teaching and learning occur through dynamic relationships: students learn from teachers, but perhaps more importantly for this age, students learn from each other.**

Knowledge building occurs when students engage in learning together. When insight is shared, understanding is strengthened. Teaching and learning occur through dynamic relationships: Students learn from teachers, but perhaps more importantly for this age, students learn from each other.

Creating an Identity-Safe Classroom

In conversations about subjects that lie close to the heart of a student's identity, clear ground rules for respect must be established. We ask students to stay open, notice their feelings, and continue processing them through talking and writing. We introduce the concept of cognitive dissonance (the tension students feel when new ideas conflict with what they previously believed to be true) to give them a vocabulary for authentic conversations that may feel awkward at first (Gorski, 2009). We encourage them to "lean into the discomfort" when challenging ideas and new feelings emerge. When students like Karla and Carlos share their personal experiences, they are often surprised by the feedback they get from their peers.

Some white students, however, feel guilt by association when hearing these stories. They may want to dismiss or deny the stories students of color tell to avoid their uncomfortable feelings. Yet when students understand that internal tension often facilitates dynamic learning, they can learn to manage the conflict produced by challenging new information. Heffernan and Lewison (2009) report that tension can be a resource for students who "consciously choose to engage with somewhat disturbing new ideas" (p. 27). We ask our students to consciously engage not only with the ideas, but also with each other as they reveal their diverse experiences. We ask them not to back away from what they honestly think and feel. We ask them to speak authentically and listen to each other respectfully. We ask them to be aware of their thoughts, feelings, and reactions, and work through their discomfort.

In a structured environment made safe for them to express their differences, students find they can be accepted and esteemed for them, rather than disparaged. When they hear other students echo ideas and feelings they themselves have been afraid to express, they realize that underneath their apparent differences, there is far more that unites than divides them. They learn that expressing, rather than suppressing, the characteristics that make them unique nurtures authentic relationships. Students benefit from direct discussions in the classroom about their personal experience with prejudice (Berrett, 2012; Cross & Strauss, 1998; Tatum, 1992). Cross and Strauss (1998) found that "rather than alienate, 'difference' is transformed into something that is accessible, friendly and engaging" (p. 275). Our students confirm this finding. "I feel more confident with my background, my personality, my character, and more confident with expressing who I am without fear of being harshly judged," Tonya wrote, "and because of that, I feel more confident in supporting others when they express certain aspects of their identity that might be different from mine."

> When they hear other students echo ideas and feelings they themselves have been afraid to express, they realize that underneath their apparent differences, there is far more that unites than divides them.

The Structure of Transformational Inquiry

The TI curriculum is divided into three main inquiry units: race, gender, and class. Each unit serves as a generative theme and follows a similar template, building instruction from the four domains: personal, social, cognitive, and action. The activities from the personal and social domains inspire students to apply themselves in the academic domain. Questions arising out of their personal stories lead them into further research, and through their natural curiosity, they learn valuable academic skills. They invariably want to take action on what they have learned. Nina, for instance, recognized her issues with low self-esteem in an article on adolescent female typecasting (Caldwell & Swift, 2003). Hearing other girls voice similar feelings and experiences fueled her passion to learn more. "I learned that so many girls feel just exactly as I do," she wrote. "It came as a shock because none of these girls should be thinking about themselves like that. Every single one of them deserves a confidence boost to match where her self-esteem should be." Subsequent to Nina's interpersonal discovery, she collaborated with Trish on a short, creative film, demonstrating the lengths girls go to in order to fit in, causes of low self-esteem, and methods girls could use to improve their self-worth. Trish and Nina's movie incorporated their own experience with interviews with their peers and knowledge they gained from academic research. They presented the film in class and circulated it on social media.

Inquiry Into Race

Race is a modern idea, historically defined by dominant groups. Racial divisions are socially imagined concepts without genetic basis (Adelman, 2003). Nineteenth-century notions of race tied skin color to traits involving intelligence, physical capacities, psychological makeup, and scales of "civilization" (Omi & Winant, 2015; Painter, 2011). Notions of race established "a rigid hierarchy of socially exclusive categories" that bolstered unequal rank and provided the rationalization for colonialism and slavery" (AAA Statement on Race, 1998). The expansion of genetic science in the twentieth century, however, debunked previously held ideas that there were distinct racial divisions within the human species. DNA analysis reveals that there is far more variation within "racial" groups (94 percent) than between them (6 percent) (AAA Statement on Race, 1998).

Racialized identities, however, yield profound material effects. A survey of United States' history—Native American genocide; slavery; Jim Crow;

debt peonage; unfair housing practices; inequitable access to banking, healthcare, and education; restrictions on citizenship and voting rights; Chinese and Japanese exclusion; internment camps; draconian immigration laws; the rise of the prison industrial complex—reveals far more about the causes and effects of racial inequities than genetic rationalizations. Learning the impact of our nation's racial history helps students understand not only the world they live in, but also themselves. When they see themselves in the context of a larger social matrix, they gain the power to depersonalize negative messages they may have internalized. They come to realize many of their struggles are social/political and not merely personal. This larger sense of identity empowers them with greater objectivity to think more clearly about the positions they hold in society. The communication skills students learn through honest conversations with each other prepare them for a changing world. To negotiate increasingly multi-ethnic communities, they need to accept and esteem cultural differences, ask questions rather than make assumptions, and learn to build relationships across difference.

> The communication skills students learn through honest conversations with each other prepare them for a changing world.

Learning to think objectively about race—to think systematically about racial inequality and to act to overcome racial injustice—requires the courage to explore one's inner landscape, examine the effects of one's cultural conditioning, and act in ways that heal rather than reinforce systemic racism. When contained within a precise and reliable communication model, conversations about race can be productive and enriching for all concerned. By laying the groundwork for an identity-safe classroom and keeping the focus on personal and felt experience, conversations that become debate oriented can be redirected. Such conversations yield profoundly unifying results.

Inquiry Into Gender

Gender, like race, is by definition a social construct. There may be biological variations, but these differentiations fall along a spectrum that doesn't divide neatly into the binary categories of male and female. Gender identity refers to an individual's relationship to the cultural concepts of masculinity and femininity, and social conditioning creates an artificial gender binary that coerces performance of prescribed roles. During adolescence, the gender police are particularly active, with gender-based harassment serving to enforce conformity. Many young men assert power by denigrating girls and harassing other males who do not conform to the conventions of masculinity. Many young women submerge their anger and act out internalized sexist oppression on each other with gossip instead of direct communication (Caldwell & Swift, 2003; Relational Aggression Overview, 2013). LGBT students face pervasive harassment with 74 percent reporting verbal harassment and 34 percent reporting physical harassment at school (The 2013 National School Climate Survey).

"Undoing gender" means young men must undo dominance, and young women must undo submissiveness. As long as the hierarchy seems "natural," it will go unquestioned. Learning to think clearly about gender involves de-normalizing sexism, heterosexism, and cissexism. When students have the opportunity to examine gender stereotypes and discuss the effects they experience in their lives, the discussion shifts to the exercise of power: Who produces these fields of identity and why? In what ways are certain bodies weighted with differential life chances? Who is empowered and who is disempowered? How is my identity shaped by society, and how can I exercise more autonomy over my identity? Given the chance to explore their feelings and share their experiences, students are quick to move beyond stereotypes. Because they already have a framework for analysis gained from the unit on race, they "get real" fast.

Inquiry Into Social Class

Like race and gender, there is no one definition of "class." Social class may be the most malleable and least visible identity in our classrooms, yet it exerts strong influence on the material and psychological lives of students. Social class affects their life opportunities in terms of health, nutrition, and education. It is not surprising that socioeconomic status is the best predictor of success in school (Putnam, 2015) because the process of schooling is itself based on class, reflecting the norms of traditional white middle-class assimilationist society (Kumashiro, 2012). Schooling, with its grades and rankings, reinforces and reproduces social class hierarchies. As Cornell West says, "Rich kids get taught, and poor kids get tested" (hooks, 2014).

A study of class begins with questioning the myth that the United States is a classless society. Students are keenly aware how they are ranked according to social class, and they talk about frequently comparing their material standing to that of others. Even affluent students feel class insecurity if their houses are not the biggest on the block. They know who wears designer labels and who wears expensive shoes. Yet most lack the vocabulary to articulate their perceptions. Terms that describe class identities—working class, middle class, owning class, underclass, blue collar, and white collar—are unfamiliar to them. They have no understanding of economic terms such as income, assets, liabilities, net worth, and gross domestic product. They have only a vague sense of how capitalism operates as an economic system or how it compares in theory and practice to other economic systems such as socialism and communism. Their emerging questions, however, open doors to academic explorations of economic systems and histories.

Learning by Design

Students' authentic questions guide the course of study. They contribute articles, invite expert speakers, submit videos for media analysis, and suggest books and movies they find inspiring. When their recommendations are integrated into the curriculum, they take ownership of learning and teach each other. They assess each other after every major project, and at the end of each semester, they assess themselves.

Conclusion

Transformational Inquiries address identity development in the context of building healthy peer relationships in a safe classroom community. To rise to the challenges of an emerging global community, students need a respectful learning environment in which they find personal expression and shared meaning. Such communities help students not only to recognize the inherent value of all humanity, but also to think critically, act rationally, and participate in a pluralistic society.

Transformational Inquiries begin in the personal realm with self-reflection and then move into sharing and mirroring each other's experiences. Reflecting on their own and each other's experiences raises self-awareness, helps them understand and respect one another, and strengthens their emerging identities. The questions raised in the process inspire curiosity about the effects of their identities. They eagerly build academic skills so they can search for answers to their questions and, consequently, take greater responsibility for their education. They learn to synthesize information and arrive at their own conclusions. As they begin to view their identities in the framework of a larger social matrix, their feelings become depersonalized, and their thinking becomes more objective. Ultimately, they are motivated to take action to affect the world they live in.

The interpersonal activities are without question the driving force of the TI method. Students report that the close relationships they create are the most important aspect of work they do with each other. "I would say I definitely learned the most from my classmates," writes Trish. "Hearing them talk and listening to their opinions meant a lot and it made it possible for me to learn things I never would have learned before." Joseph, who once felt alienated from his peers during group projects, writes: "I feel like I have much stronger bonds with many people in the class and feel like I can trust them more." Amanda writes, "With friends from other areas of my life, such as neighbors or teammates, I could never talk about the sincere and risky topics we discuss in class." She goes on to say that learning about the effects of discrimination on the friends she has come to know in the class "makes me want to take action even more." These personal connections make social justice meaningful. "I hadn't understood how much prejudice still exists in today's society," Amanda continues, "when I thought of racism or sexism, I thought of slavery and historical oppression. Now I see oppression every day in the media, society, and on occasion, in this school."

The recursive nature of the curriculum allows students to draw parallels and see intersections between different kinds of oppression. Joshua, initially entrenched in defensiveness when we began talking about race, asked, "Why are white males always the bad guys?" By the beginning of the unit on social class, Joshua was identifying not only social structures that keep oppression in place, but also recognizing the detrimental effects white privilege has had on his own sense of identity. Joshua emerged from the class committed to social justice.

Because TI is tied to current issues and evolving theoretical ideas, it continues to grow and change, but certain aspects of it stay the same. In a rapidly changing world, there are some constants: the love of discovery, the power of authentic communication, and the generosity of respect for others. Because TI is bound to these human characteristics, it provides a method through which differences can be transcended and community established. Authentic inquiry flourishes and skill building emerges as natural byproducts of real-life learning. By providing a forum to engage them and a template to guide them, we bear witness to our students' ever-emerging identities and phenomenal growth.

References

AAA statement on race. (1998). American anthropological association executive board. *American Anthropologist*, 100(3), 712–713.

Adelman, L. (2003). *Race: The power of an illusion*. California Newsreel/PBS.

Apple, M. (2004). *Ideology and Curriculum*. New York: RoutledgeFalmer. (Kindle Version). Retrieved from Amazon.com.

Barron, B. & Darling-Hammond, L. (2008). Teaching for meaningful learning: A review of research on inquiry-based and cooperative learning. *Powerful learning: What we know about teaching for understanding*. New York: John Wiley & Sons.

Baxter Magolda, M. (1999). *Creating Contexts for Learning and Self-Authorship: Constructive developmental pedagogy*. Nashville, TN: Vanderbilt University Press.

Berrett, D. (2012, Nov 19). Encounters with diversity, on campuses and in coursework, bolsters critical-thinking skills. *The Chronicle of Higher Education*. Retrieved from http://chronicle.com/article/Diversity-Bolsters/135858/.

Cabrera, N. L., Milem, J. F., & Marx, R. W. (2012). *An Empirical Analysis of the Effects of Mexican American Studies Participation on Student Achievement within Tucson Unified School District*. Tucson, AZ: Report to Special Master Dr. Willis D. Hawley on the Tucson Unified School District Desegregation Case.

Caldwell, M. (2012). Inquiry into identity: Teaching critical thinking through a study in race, class and gender. *Middle School Journal*, 43(6), 6–15.

Caldwell, M. & Swift, J. (2003). Beyond "mean girl" typecasting: Power, popularity and potential. *Schoolbook: A Journal of Education*, 12(2), 3–8.

Clifford, P. & Marinucci, S. (2008). Testing the waters: Three elements of classroom inquiry. *Harvard Educational Review*, 78(4), 675–688.

Cross, W. Jr. & Strauss, L. (1998). The Everyday Functions of African American Identity. In J. Swim & C. Stangor (Eds.), *Prejudice: The target's perspective* (pp. 268–278). Maryland Heights, MO: Academic Press.

Duncan-Andrade, J. M. & Morrell, E. (2008). *The Art of Critical Pedagogies: Possibilities for moving from theory to practice in urban schools*. New York: Peter Lang.

Friere, Paulo (1970). *Pedagogy of the Oppressed*. New York: The Seabury Press.

Gorski, P. (2009). Cognitive dissonance as a strategy in social justice teaching. *Multicultural Education*, 17(1), 54–57.

Gurin, P., Dey, E. L., Hurtado, S., & Gurin, G. (2002). Diversity and higher education: Theory and impact on learning outcomes. *Harvard Educational Review*, 72(3), 330–366.

Harper, B. & Tuckman, B. (2006). Racial identity beliefs and academic achievement: Does being black hold students back? *Social Psychology of Education*, 9(4), 381–403.

Heffernan, L. & Lewison, M. (2009). Keep your eyes on the prize: Critical stance in the middle school classroom. *Voices from the Middle*, 17(2), 19–27.

hooks, b. (1994). *Teaching to Transgress: Education as the practice of freedom*. New York: Routledge.

hooks, b. (2014, Oct 10). Transgressions. Scholar-in-Residence Program, Eugene Lang College of Liberal Arts, The New School, New York. Retrieved from www.you tube.com/watch?v=_LL0k6_pPKw&feature=youtu.be.

Kumashiro, K. (2012). *Bad Teacher! How blaming teachers distorts the bigger picture*. New York: Teachers College Press.

Omi, M. & Winant, H. (2015) *Racial Formations in the Unites States* (3rd ed.). New York: Routledge.

Painter, N. I. (2011). *The History of White People*. New York: W. W. Norton & Company.

Pelligrino, J. W. & Hilton. M. L. (Eds.). (2012). *Education for Life and Work: Developing transferable knowledge and skills in the twenty-first century*. Washington, DC: National Academies Press.

Putnam, R. D. (2015). *Our Kids: The American dream in crisis*. New York: Simon & Schuster. (Kindle version). Retrieved from Amazon.com.

Relational Aggression Overview (2013). *The Ophelia Project*. Retrieved from www.opheliaproject.org/facts/RelationalAggressionOverview.pdf.

Richardson, S. T., Sinclair, K. O., Poteat, V. P., & Koenig, B. W. (2012). Adolescent health and harassment based on discriminatory bias. *American Journal of Public Health, 102*(3), 493–495.

Romero, A., Arce, S., & Cammarota, J. (2009, Jul). A Barrio pedagogy: Identity, intellectualism, activism, and academic achievement through the evolution of critically compassionate intellectualism. *Race, Ethnicity and Education, 12*(2), 217–233.

Roseberry, A., McIntyre, E., & Gonzalez, N. (2001). *Classroom Diversity: Connecting curriculum to students' lives*. Portsmouth, NH: Heinemann.

Shor, I. (1992). *Empowering Education: Critical teaching for social change*. Chicago, IL: University of Chicago Press.

Shor, I. (1999). What is critical literacy? *Journal of Pedagogy, Pluralism and Practice, 1*(4). Retrieved from www.lesley.edu/journal-pedagogy-pluralism-practice/ira-shor/critical-literacy/.

Steele, D. & Cohn-Vargas, B. (2013). *Identity Safe Classrooms: Places to belong and learn*. Thousand Oaks, CA: Corwin.

Sturrock, J. (Ed.). (1979). *Structuralism and Since: From Levi-Strauss to Derrida*. Oxford: Oxford University Press.

Tatum, B. D. (1992). Talking about race, learning about racism: The application of racial identity development theory in the classroom. *Harvard Educational Review, 62*(1), 1–24.

The 2013 National School Climate Survey. (2013). *Gay, Lesbian & Straight Education Network* (GLSEN). Retrieved from www.glsen.org/article/2013-national-school-climate-survey.

Toomey, R. & Umana-Taylor, A. (2012). The role of ethnic identity on self-esteem for ethnic minority youth: A brief review. *Prevention Researcher, 19*(2), 8–12.

Valenzuela, A. (1999). *Subtractive Schooling*. Albany, NY: State University of New York Press.

Wink, J. (2005). *Critical Pedagogy: Notes from the real world*. Boston, MA: Pearson Education, Inc.

Wortham, S. (2006). *Learning Identity: The joint emergence of social identification and academic learning*. New York: Cambridge University Press.

2

Transformational Inquiry: Foundations for Practice

Colby, a hearing-impaired student, sits alone outside the circle every day. He wants a friend more than anything in the world, but because he was bullied in third grade, he is so afraid of rejection that he keeps everyone at arm's length. Marcia bosses the boys around to cover up the vulnerability she feels. She pretends to be tough so the jokes they make about her body don't hurt as much. Cameron, excluded in fourth grade by the popular clique, waits quietly for someone to reach out to her, because she is too afraid to reach out to anyone herself. Timothy thinks he might be gay and is afraid his friends will reject him if they find out. Mariana has been sleeping on a mattress with her two sisters in the living room of a neighbor's house since her family was evicted. Jennifer's parents went through a difficult divorce last year, and now she lives between their two houses. She's embarrassed that her family isn't "normal like everyone else's." Travis's mother was recently diagnosed with cancer, and he regrets that when she tried to hug him in front of his friends, he pushed her away. He didn't want the guys to think he was a little kid.

Every classroom contains a diverse mix of individuals, no matter what the demographic makeup of the group. Each student comes with a unique perspective colored by a distinct family and cultural background. They arrive with different levels of maturity and widely diverse learning styles. Most of them are grappling to form stable identities. They are struggling to discover who they are and define who they want to become. Their race, gender, and class identities are crucial components in their emerging senses of self. They want to learn about themselves and each other, and their diverse identities provide the potential for dynamic learning.

Wortham (2006) reminds us that social identification and academic learning are inextricably bound, so strengthening students' personal and collective identities strengthens their capacity to learn. When their lives are the subject of study, a sense of interrelatedness in the classroom transfers to greater engagement and motivation to learn (Baxter Magolda, 1999; Friere, 1970; Shor, 1992; Wink, 2005). Research shows that culturally relevant curricula combined with identity exploration results in dramatic increases in school achievement for at-risk students (Dee & Penner, 2016). Hammon (2015) belives culturally responive teaching can close achievement gaps. Privileged students also benefit from making emotional connections and building relationships in diverse groups (Swalwell, 2015). We see rapid personal, social, and intellectual development in our students—stronger relationships, closer collaboration, increased motivation, more thorough research, improved writing skills, greater facility with technology, and a developing framework for self-assessment.

A Critical Window of Opportunity

Adolescence offers an unparalleled window of opportunity because individuals are more sensitive to their environments than they will be at any other time in their lives (Erikson, 1968; Phinney & Ong, 2007; Steinberg, 2014). Erikson (1968) viewed identity formation as a reflexive process between personal consciousness and the social environment. Personal identity, or the perception of "self-sameness" over time, goes hand in hand with this self-sameness being recognized by others (p. 50). He believed human development contains certain potentials and limitations that can be actualized at specific points, but only if environmental conditions facilitate them. He viewed adolescence as one such opportunity and believed schools could provide environments that strengthened students' identities.

Recent research in neuroscience validates Erikson's views on the critical window of opportunity in adolescence (Steinberg, 2014). As the prefrontal cortex matures, unused neurons and their connections are pruned away, while neural networks more frequently used are strengthened. In other words, brain pathways more frequently activated determine the structure of the adult brain. According to Steinberg (2014), the adolescent brain is particularly sensitive to environmental influences, especially regions of the prefrontal cortex, which governs executive function, decision-making, self-control, and moral reasoning. "The brain will never again be as plastic as it is during adolescence," he says. "We cannot afford to squander this second opportunity to help young people be happier, healthier, and more successful. Adolescence is our last best chance to make a difference" (p. 217). Willis (2011), as well, issues a call to teachers to take advantage of this critical window of neurological development. She sees teachers as "critical nurturers" of brain development, who as such, "define the qualities students bring with them into their adult lives" (p. 259). The environments we create in our classrooms and how we ask our students to use their brains during this critical window may advance or inhibit their adult reasoning capacity.

> The environments we create in our classrooms and how we ask our students to use their brains during this critical window may advance or inhibit their adult reasoning capacity.

Identity Formation

Personal and social identities are analytically distinct but interrelated concepts. Personal identity is a subjective sense of self, while social identity is frequently an assigned category (particularly when bodily attributes such as skin color or secondary sex characteristics make it visible). Erikson (1968) understood that identity formation is complicated by status differences based on race, class, gender, and age, and that these differences produce material as well as psychological effects. The political dimensions of social identity complicate identity formation and invite analysis of privilege, oppression, and justice.

Côté and Levine (2002) define agency as intentional action for the purpose of altering the social environment. Individuals with greater agency have the capacity to resist or act back on coercive social structures that impinge on their identities. Agency is associated with self-esteem, a sense of purpose in life (p. 149) and increased capacity for self-determination. Because some social identities carry more influence than others, the development of agency is not just a personal process. For devalued social groups, internalizing negative self-images (believing negative stereotypes about one's self are true) can result in self-denigration (Evans, Foreney, Guido, Patton & Renn, 2010). For dominant groups, internalizing negative stereotypes about others results in

> The more conscious individuals become of the ongoing reciprocal dynamic between the self and its environment, the more empowered they become to exercise agency to create change.

bias, whether conscious or unconscious. In both cases, these unexamined mindsets are based on miseducation and interfere with the development of agency.

These mindsets, however, are not immutable and can be transformed through a process of questioning, social reflection, and knowledge building. People either buy into oppressive mindsets without question, or they exercise their agency to challenge and transform them. The more conscious individuals become of the ongoing reciprocal dynamic between the self and its environment, the more empowered they become to exercise agency to create change (Figure 2.1).

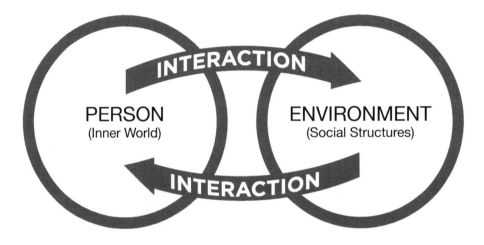

- Person projects sense of self into their environment.
- Environment reflects an image of the self back.
- Person adapts sense of self to fit the environment's reflection, or if identity is strong enough, uses agency to change the environment.

Figure 2.1 Identity formation as a dynamic, interactive relationship between the person and the environment

Identity Exploration: From Clueless to Crisis to Commitment

Models of social identity formation patterns have been developed for specific groups, including African Americans, Asians, Hispanics, Native Americans, whites, women, sexual orientation, and ethnic identities (ACT for Youth Center of Excellence, 2016; Evans et al., 2010). These models, though differing in design (number and descriptions of stages, phases, orientations, or statuses) and in application to specific social identities, nonetheless, suggest that individuals across cultures move through somewhat similar phases in their quests to construct viable identities. The trajectory involves movement from a naïve state (in which identity is unquestioned) to a period of self-exploration (characterized by conflict and searching) to a place of identity commitment (distinguished by resolution of conflict). None of these models suggest that this trajectory is a linear process, but rather reiterative and cyclic. Nor do they suggest that an ideal identity is ultimately achieved but that identity construction and reconstruction continues over a lifetime. Nonetheless, psychological health (Berry, 2005) and greater self-determination (Côté & Levine, 2002; Erikson, 1968; Evans et al., 2010; Kohlberg, 1976) are associated with the committed identity stages.

Naïve and Unquestioning. The naïve stage is characteristic of childhood but not limited to childhood. Children accept their socially ascribed identities (sometimes including negative stereotypes) as correct representations of themselves, taking their cues from what they have learned from parents, religion, school, the media, or peers. They may not notice or feel impacted by differences. Krista, the only African American student in her peer group, for instance, told the class that race was not an important part of her identity. Perhaps she could not safely explore her racial identity without jeopardizing her place among her white friends. Or she may have been confident enough in her identity that she did not need to explore it. Either way, she did not choose to explore this aspect of her identity in our class but instead chose to explore other aspects of her identity such as religion and gender.

Problems arise, however, when conflict about social identity is submerged below the level of consciousness. Members of devalued social groups may disidentify with their own group and instead identify with the dominant culture in an attempt to gain status (French, Seidman, Allen & Aber, 2006). This can result in internalizing negative stereotypes about their group, which in turn can produce negative self-images. Aida, a transnational adoptee, looked back on her naïve status from a place of exploration:

> As a child I used to hide my language. When people would speak to me in the Ethiopian language, I would say, "I'm sorry, I don't speak Amharic." This was the small assimilating child speaking. Back then it was a lie, but today I honestly have forgotten the language and it has been my greatest loss. The fact that I was ashamed to be anything but American like everyone else, gives me much regret.

Women in the naïve stage may prefer male bosses because they believe women to be less capable of leadership. Blacks may deny the effects of systemic racism and attribute the academic achievement gap to laziness or poor parenting. Whites may believe they are successful because of a superior work ethic, or due to individual merit, and blame other groups for "bringing their problems on themselves," insisting that they "pull themselves up by their bootstraps." Men may make crude jokes about women in positions of power. Heterosexuals may see homosexuality as unnatural or deviant.

The Age of Exploration. During adolescent identity exploration, young people question who they are, what others think of them, and how they fit in to the larger social picture. When how they see themselves does not match how others perceive them, inner conflict may result. The exploration phase is unique for each individual, but generalizations have been made across social identity groups. For individuals with devalued social identities (women, people of color, the poor, LGBT students), the exploration phase can be catalyzed by an encounter with injustice. Cassidy, a student of color, believed her science teacher did not consider her as capable as some of the white students in her class. She felt misjudged and unrecognized. Her inner sense of self did not match up with the image the teacher reflected back to her, so she had to struggle to resolve this inner conflict. For dominant groups, identity exploration can begin through a gradual recognition that all social statuses are not considered equal and may be the result of education or hearing about the experiences of others. Karen, a white student wrote:

> When I heard about cops stopping people or people being watched in stores because of their race, that was a time when I really realized how much unfair privilege I possess, just because of my race, and I understood so much more what some people have to go through.

The exploration phase has emotional, intellectual, and ethical dimensions. Identity exploration is associated with openness and curiosity but also with increased levels of anxiety and depression (Schwartz, Zamboanga, Weisskirch & Rodriguez, 2009). The experience of "waking up to injustice" can be intensely emotional. For devalued groups, recognizing and making meaning of racism or sexism is a "significant developmental task" (Torres & Hernandez, 2007). For dominant groups, being identified with the oppressor creates an ethical dilemma. Identity exploration carries a sense of risk for all adolescents, who must leave a stable identity behind and explore new territory both psychologically and socially (Evans et al., 2010; Schwartz et al., 2009). Moving through exploration toward an integrated identity requires the capacity for self-reflection, self-regulation, and self-discipline (Flum & Kaplan, 2006). Students benefit, not only from the support of teachers and peers, but also through channeling their emotional energy into intellectual projects that help them express a positive sense of self.

Members of devalued groups may go through periods of defining themselves in opposition to dominant groups and seeking solace in relationships with members of their own groups in order to strengthen their identities. They may feel anger at dominant groups, as well as at members of their own group they see as colluding with the system. They may feel guilt that they cannot stand up to injustice or fear that if they do, they will be rejected. They may feel invisible, unrecognized, or misjudged. They need a safe place to process their feelings with people they know will understand. They gravitate toward members of their own social identity group because they can relate through common experiences and ways of knowing. These students need teachers who share their social identities to mirror their feelings and reassure them of their worth.

Dominant groups in the exploration stage may feel anger, guilt, and shame as they come to see their group as perpetrating systems of oppression. They may engage in intense self-examination to identify patterns of oppression in their group and in themselves. They may initially deny membership in their own group, preferring to think they are "not like the others." They struggle with wanting to "help" but cannot yet see how to be in equal relationships with members of other groups. Their focus gradually shifts from the problems of target groups to the problems in their own group.

In the intellectual dimension of the exploration stage, students are motivated to learn. Intellectual exploration provides relief from emotional intensity as cognitive processing helps them temper and integrate their feelings. Students of color may be motivated to learn more about their history and reclaim appreciation for their heritage and culture, thereby developing a sense of self and group pride. Young women frequently seek role models who have overcome sexism and want to learn everything they can to bolster their self-esteem. White students move through guilt by learning about white racial justice advocates and coming to understand that whiteness is an ideology, not a skin color. When young men realize the harm sexism causes, not just to women, but also to them, they want to learn how they can change things. For all students, seeing the intersecting oppressions between groups helps them identify the ways they have been hurt, as well as the ways they may have hurt others.

> **For all students, seeing the intersecting oppressions between groups helps them identify the ways they have been hurt, as well as the ways they may have hurt others.**

Identity exploration also has an ethical dimension. Students want to be good people; they want to make the world a better place. For Erikson (1968, p. 39), "An ethical capacity is the true criteria of identity." He saw identity and morality as inextricably linked with integrity being the end point of development. Kohlberg's (1976) model suggests that individuals complete the exploration phase at different times and to varying degrees. Most people in his study remained at a conventional stage of moral development with limited agency, while only a minority progressed to the principle-based, post-conventional level at which critical analysis operates.

Re-integration and Commitment. Individuals emerge from the exploration phase with more fluid and multidimensional senses of identity. They possess a better grasp of the interrelatedness of various aspects of their identity and a more expansive view of themselves. They feel greater confidence and pride in their social group. They realize they must necessarily function within systems of social oppression, but they consciously seek strategies to mitigate the systemic effects. In this stage, members of devalued groups still maintain their in-group relationships for ongoing support, but they are also ready to form relationships with select dominant group members. They may form alliances with other social identity groups to create strategies and exchange mutual support. Dominant group members who reach the integration stage have learned to appreciate positive aspects of their identities without feeling superior. They have moved through feelings of guilt and are ready to take action to address social problems in alliance with other groups. Whites can be antiracist; heterosexuals can support LGBT rights; and men can promote the advancement of women and girls.

For all social groups, this stage is characterized by a commitment to something larger than themselves: to advancing their social identity group or to social justice in general. The re-integration stage is characteristic of adulthood in that one's identity becomes connected to a larger sense of purpose in life. Social identity commitment has been related to increased self-esteem (Phinney, Cantu & Kurtz, 1997; Toomey & Umana-Taylor, 2012; Umana-Taylor & Updegraff, 2007), emotional stability (Crocetti, Rubini, Luyckx & Meeus, 2007), and greater psychological health (Berry, 2005). A strong sense of self provides sustenance to prevail in the face of discrimination as well as the motivation to act on behalf of social change.

Scaffolding Instruction Through the Four Domains

Transformational Inquiry (TI) scaffolds identity exploration through four domains of learning: personal, social, cognitive, and action (Figure 2.2). These four categories are analytical distinctions that help us think about how students learn, but in reality, these domains are overlapping and inter-related. Learning does not progress linearly from the personal to the social to the cognitive to the action domain, but instead involves a recursive process with each domain affecting the other three to build integrated identity-based learning.

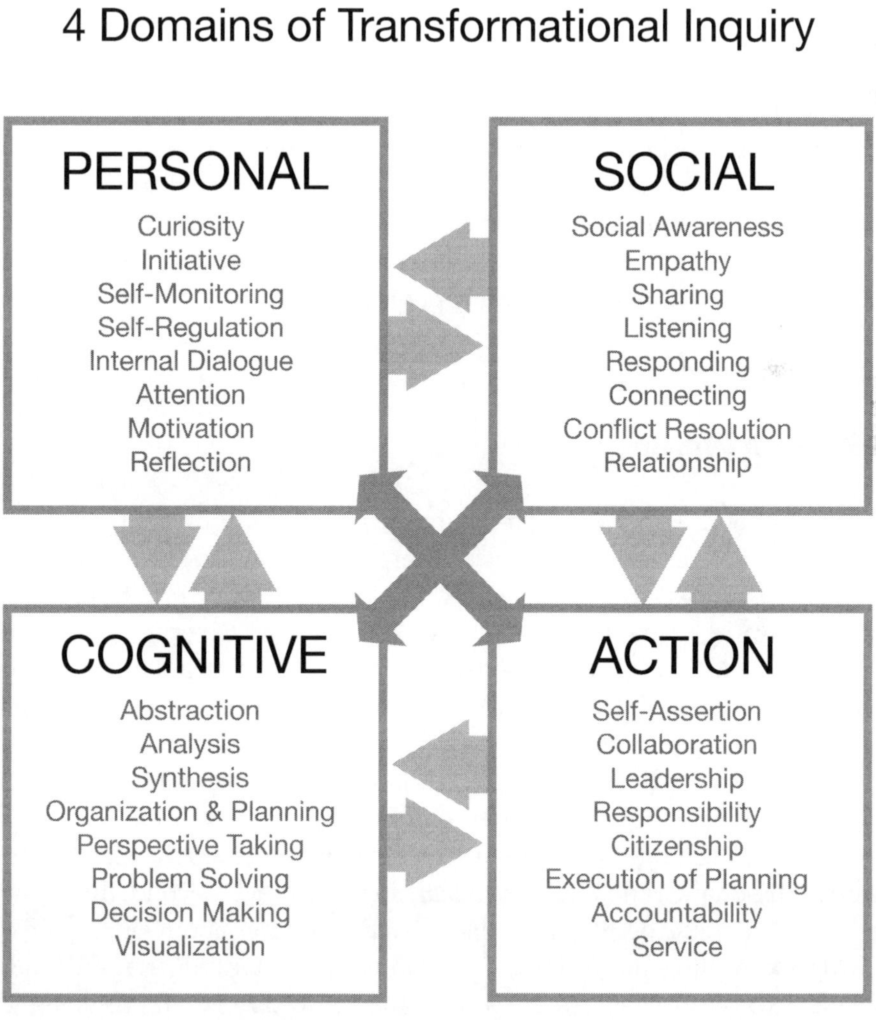

4 Domains of Transformational Inquiry

PERSONAL	SOCIAL
Curiosity	Social Awareness
Initiative	Empathy
Self-Monitoring	Sharing
Self-Regulation	Listening
Internal Dialogue	Responding
Attention	Connecting
Motivation	Conflict Resolution
Reflection	Relationship

COGNITIVE	ACTION
Abstraction	Self-Assertion
Analysis	Collaboration
Synthesis	Leadership
Organization & Planning	Responsibility
Perspective Taking	Citizenship
Problem Solving	Execution of Planning
Decision Making	Accountability
Visualization	Service

Figure 2.2 Domains of Transformational Inquiry

The goal of TI is not to change or shape an individual's identity but rather to facilitate reflection that strengthens and broadens it. Helping students build strong identities helps them learn. In the process of identity exploration, students gain capacity for self-regulation (Flum & Kaplan, 2006), perspective taking, and critical thinking (Berrett, 2012; Biren, Gurin & Lopez, 2003). Strong identities correlate not only with increased self-esteem and academic achievement but also with greater capacity for self-determination (Côté & Levine, 2002; Erikson, 1968; Evans et al., 2010; Kohlberg, 1976).

> . . . students are capable of processing powerful feelings and using them to gain insight about the world they live in and their place in it. Indeed, they have to if they want to evolve into capable adults.

Students frequently undergo transformations in their thinking in a TI classroom. Laura, a white student who thought racism went out with the Civil Rights Movement in the sixties, was in for an awakening. Tiffany, a high-achieving African American student, had denied the existence of racism in her life, and facing the effects of injustice was painful. When students explore their identities, their feelings may initially intensify. But students are capable of processing powerful feelings and using them to gain insight about the world they live in and their place in it. Indeed, they have to if they want to evolve into capable adults.

The Personal Domain

Self-exploration begins with self-attunement or attention to felt experience, including bodily sensations, physical energy, feelings, thoughts, preferences, curiosity, opinions, and ideas. Research on the role of emotional awareness in learning shows clear benefits (Brackett & Rivers, 2014; Durlak, Domitrovich, Weissberg & Gullotta, 2015). First, self-attunement increases capacity for self-regulation, a skill Steinberg (2014) sees as the most crucial skill adolescents can develop because it strengthens executive function and builds connection in the brain's prefrontal cortex. Self-regulation is important for impulse control, but also for maintaining the degree of inner equilibrium that enhances learning. Increasing affective awareness helps students manage cognitive dissonance and counteract learning resistance. Second, inner awareness develops metacognition, or the capacity to think about one's thinking. Metacognition plays an important role in abstract thinking, self-evaluation, and social development. As adolescents learn to observe themselves, they become aware of how others perceive them and can monitor their behavior accordingly. Third, attention to felt experience increases awareness of preference, an important component of decision-making. Emotional awareness is crucial to motivation, because when feelings become self-directed, individuals move into conscious action. When students understand their own motivations, they are also in a better position to understand others. They develop the capacity to read others' emotions through body language, facial expressions, and tone of voice, and thus, they are better able to evaluate social situations.

Inquiry into the personal realm is guided by the questions "Who am I?" "What do I know?" "How do I feel?" "What am I afraid of?" "Who do I love?" "What do I hope for?" "What is my experience?" "What challenges have I faced?" "What do I want to know?" "What do I believe?" Students explore these questions through contemplation, reflective writing, self-surveys, and other activities designed to stimulate self-study.

The Social Domain

Adolescents feel an urgent drive to connect with peers through social relationships. Noam and Fiore (2004) write: "Human beings learn and grow not in isolation but through interaction with each other" (p. 12). Students learn through connections they make with teachers, but equally important, they learn through relationships with each other. Strengthening peer relationships satisfies a key developmental need: belongingness (Hazen, Schlozman & Beresin, 2008; Noam, 1999; *At the Turning Point, n.d.*). If the need to belong is met, students thrive. If not, they attempt to fit in in unhealthy ways: bullying, trying to be "cool," complying with peer pressure, or kowtowing to stereotypes. Reluctant to express their individuality for fear of ridicule, they over-conform, which creates an inner disconnect, as it requires ignoring, avoiding, or shutting down authentic feelings. Superficial cognitive processing, apathy, and lack of interest in school are the results.

Siegel (2013) describes "feeling felt" as the sense of being deeply understood by another person, an experience that results in secure attachments and increases capacity for self-regulation. Because social recognition plays a crucial role in identity formation, students need to see a healthy sense of who they are reflected back to them. When they exchange stories and experience empathetic feedback, they make deeper connections that counteract social insecurities. In the safety of the classroom, they become more open to expressing their individuality and more capable of self-defining. "Since the course I feel more open to say what's on my mind and stand up for what's right and not do what everyone else is doing," writes Jeremy.

In a nation divided by demographics, conversations about identity can be emotionally charged. When students share experiences of bigotry or exclusion, their emotional lives move into the forefront. Students of color share stories of being treated with suspicion by clerks in stores and not having their intelligence recognized. Girls share the pressure they feel to identify with their appearance and the need to be perfect. Boys describe pressure to demean girls to protect themselves from being called "gay" or ridiculed for not being "manly" enough.

In the social domain, teachers model and provide instruction for healthy communication skills: attentive and respectful listening, authentic self-disclosure, and supportive feedback. They provide a framework for community building, identity exploration, and identity safety. Most importantly, they see their students as good people and help them frame their identities in a positive light. Teachers recognize their students' courage, emphasize their strengths, and reflect back to them their highest potential. Students learn from teachers how to do the same for each other.

> Teachers recognize their students' courage, emphasize their strengths, and reflect back to them their highest potential. Students learn from teachers how to do the same for each other.

Before students can understand social theory, histories, politics, and current events, they must first learn to honor their subjective experience, as well as that of others. As Sarah writes, "The relationships I formed were very strong and they really affected my learning because it was safe to say what you felt and what you thought and people encouraged you and helped you along." She describes her thinking as "so much more open and bigger" as a result. For Marcus, the course "increased my ability to think about things from everyone's perspective and not just mine." Their comments reveal these mutual connections to be among the most meaningful experiences they have had in school.

The Cognitive Domain

Adolescents are funny, intellectually curious, imaginative, and, when engaged, eager to learn. They are developing the capacity for abstract reasoning and critical thinking. Literal thinkers are learning to think in symbols, understand metaphors, make analogies, see patterns, extrapolate information from one situation to another, and solve problems. Their thinking is becoming more complex, and they need challenging curricula through which they can experience achievement, accomplishment, and success in school. Ultimately, they need to find an intrinsic sense of joy in learning.

The role of the teacher in the cognitive domain is to help them extrapolate their insights about relational dynamics to understand power and politics in the wider world. To relate students' identity experiences to academic content, teachers provide reading materials with multiple perspectives and offer multicultural texts. They teach reading, writing, and research skills. They help students formulate questions and narrow topics for research. They help them find sources. They help students identify patterns and see social constructs that had previously been invisible to them. They connect current social problems to their historical roots, guide media analysis, and relate student identities to what is going on in the world through current events. They ask good questions. Equally important, they share in the excitement of learning.

The Action Domain

Themes of justice and fairness resonate strongly with young people. They are keenly aware of injustice, intensely curious about the politics going on around them, and have a strong desire to act upon the world they live in. Not satisfied to merely learn about injustice, they want to *do* something. They need to participate in solutions. Their moral development in this stage can be characterized by "a desire to make the world a better place" (*At the Turning Point*, n.d., p. 18). In identity formation, action externalizes identity through self-assertion, leadership, and community membership. Choosing actions requires an exploration of personal values, and students gain a sense of themselves based in integrity and service. Researching actions others have taken expands their perspectives and offers a lens through which they can see themselves as connected to larger social movements.

> In the face of seemingly over-whelming social justice issues, taking action empowers students by demonstrating that they can, in fact, make a difference.

Taking action completes the learning cycle, integrating the personal, social, and cognitive domains in the service of personal and social change. Action is the antidote to helplessness, isolation, and despair. Tatum (1992) considers it unethical to raise students' awareness of injustice without also raising their awareness about possibilities for change. In the face of seemingly overwhelming social justice issues, taking action empowers students by demonstrating that they can, in fact, make a difference.

Teachers provide frameworks for students to apply what they are learning in practice. Action can mean standing up to injustice or supporting a friend. It can involve speech acts, games, drama, art, music, role-playing, or writing. It can take the form of political organizing, inviting guest speakers to class, or contributing a current events story. Teachers can introduce social movements to exemplify effective action and help connect students with service organizations for participatory action projects.

Sometimes the actions students take reflect their own identity issues, but sometimes projects emerge from relationships formed between students. Michael, a white student, was deeply moved by Carlos's story about emigrating from Mexico with his mother. Carlos had shared the financial hardship his family faced, how hard his mother worked cleaning houses, and his fear that any member of his family could be deported. When it was time to choose an action project, Michael asked Carlos if they could work together on a project about immigration detention in Georgia. Carlos agreed, and they invited Vicente, another Mexican American student, to join them. Vicente was familiar with the detention process from personal experience. His father had been deported when he was eight-years-old, and he had also visited his uncle in a detention facility. Carlos, Vicente, and Michael read about the detention and deportation process in Georgia, and learned about the effects of Georgia's draconian immigration laws on undocumented workers as well as on Georgia's economy. They connected with several groups that addressed immigrant rights in Georgia and interviewed activists. They made a documentary featuring interviews with Mexican immigrants about why they came to the United States, letting their stories demonstrate what they had learned about the effects of globalism on the Mexican economy. They showed the video to the class, distributed it on social media, and sent copies to the activist groups they had interviewed.

How Educators Can Respond

Committed identities are constructed through the exploration process, and the results are greater autonomy, agency, and self-determination (Baxter Magolda, 1999; Côté & Levine, 2010; Marcia, 1993). Flum and Kaplan (2006) echo Erikson's (1968) view that schools should provide contexts for identity formation and believe providing social contexts for identity exploration to be the most important goal of education. In a rapidly changing world where self-directed learning is becoming increasingly important, they believe students should:

. . . intentionally and consciously examine, investigate, and evaluate the relevance and meaning of content and action to their sense of who they are and who they want to be, at the same time engaging in constructing and reconstructing these self-perceptions and self-definitions.

(p. 102)

Biren, Gurin, and Lopez (2003) demonstrated that higher order thinking skills increased after students engaged in structured interactions in diverse groups. They join other educators in encouraging practices that help students consider multiple perspectives and engage in social justice actions to prepare them for citizenship in a pluralistic democracy.

Steele and Cohn-Vargas (2013) emphasize the importance of classroom practices that address stereotype threat, an identity-related phenomenon that refers to the psychological risk marginalized students experience when a situation evokes the expectation of poor performance. Research indicates stereotype threat has profound effects on learning and achievement, especially among students in vulnerable social identity groups (Stroessner & Good, n.d.). For students whose intelligence has been negatively stereotyped (African Americans, Latinos, students from low socioeconomic backgrounds, women in math), fear of fulfilling the stereotype can interfere with cognitive function and result in lower performance. Students under stereotype threat may distance themselves from their identity group to avoid being stereotyped, spend less time preparing for a task, or deny the task's importance to avoid a sense of failure. Stereotype threat can result in altered identities and inhibited aspirations. Thirteen-year-old Marcia describes the effect of stereotype threat on her identity as a girl:

Creeping down the hall crowded with boys, I feel less than every single one of them. When a boy calls me a bitch because I tell him to stop bullying, I feel like I might actually be one. I swallow my words, turn them inward against myself. I have to work to remember that I am just as good.

Teachers can address stereotype threat through direct instruction, so students understand how stereotype threat functions and how it may affect them. They can introduce role models who counter negative stereotypes. They can affirm students' identities and reassure them they are capable, paying close attention to students with vulnerable social identities. They can set up environments in which students learn to validate each other through affirming, accepting, and encouraging their social identities. Honest, supportive peer feedback helps remove some of the pressure of stereotype threat. Davis, Aronson, and Salinas (2006) call on schools to create environments that lower stereotype threat through programs that promote connections between identity and academics. Such programs would "debunk the myth that Blacks do not do well in, or care about, school and allow others to maintain their ties to their cultural peer group as well as attempt to excel academically" (p. 415).

Conclusion

Adolescents are engaged in a dynamic process of identity formation. Some are doing it with a good bit of assistance from the adults around them, while others may be doing it entirely alone. They are constructing their identities in a reflexive relationship with the environments they find themselves in, largely due to the circumstances of their births. Their environments mirror back to them images of themselves, which influence who they may become. To the extent that their environments nurture and affirm their identities, they grow strong. To the extent that their environments negate and devalue them, they struggle.

  bell hooks (2015) understands conversation as "the revolutionary way of learning." She affirms that individuals can "re-vision" themselves through reflexive participation in reciprocal, dynamic relationships, a process that "liberates consciousness for a new world" through the "counter hegemonic" practice of love. TI relies on the concept that love underlies all learning. In the personal domain, love takes the form of self-respect and integrity. In the social domain, it manifests as the drive for supportive, authentic relationships. In the cognitive domain, love manifests as the intrinsic desire to know and the fulfillment of joy in learning. In the action realm, love's insistence on the alignment between integrity and action is the impetus for personal growth and social transformation.

References

ACT for Youth Center of Excellence. (2016). *Cornell University Bronfenbrenner Center for Translational Research*. Retrieved from www.actforyouth.net.

At the turning point: The young adolescent learner. (n.d.). Center for Collaborative Education. Retrieved from www.turningpts.org/pdf/YALGuide2.pdf.

Baxter Magolda, M. B. (1999). *Creating Contexts for Learning and Self-Authorship: Constructive-developmental pedagogy*. Nashville, TN: Vanderbilt University Press.

Berrett, D. (2012, Nov 19). Encounters with diversity, on campuses and in coursework, bolsters critical-thinking skills. *The Chronicle of Higher Education*. Retrieved from http://chronicle.com/article/Diversity-Bolsters/135858/.

Berry, J. W. (2005). Acculturation: Living successfully in two cultures. *International Journal of Intercultural Relationships, 29*, 697–712.

Biren, A., Gurin, P., & Lopez, G. (2003, Jul). Transformative pedagogy for democracy and social justice. *Race, Ethnicity and Education, 6*(2), 165–191.

Brackett, M. A. & Rivers, S. E. (2014). Transforming Students' Lives With Social Emotional Learning. In P. S. Alexander, R. Pekrun, & L. Linnenbrink-Garcia (Eds.), *International handbook of emotions in education*. New York: Routledge Handbooks Online.

Côté, J. E. & Levine, C. G. (2002). *Identity Formation, Agency, and Culture: A social psychological synthesis*. London: Lawrence Erlbaum Associates.

Crocetti, E., Rubini, M., Luyckx, K., & Meeus, W. H. (2007). Identity formation in early and middle adolescents from various ethnic groups: From three dimensions to five statuses. *Journal of Youth and Adolescence, 37*(8), 983–996.

Davis, C., Aronson, J., & Salinas, M. (2006). Shades of threat: Racial identity as a moderator of stereotype threat. *Journal of Black Psychology, 32*(4), 394–417.

Dee, T. & Penner, E. (2016). The causal effects of cultural relevance: Evidence from an ethnic studies curriculum. *CEPA Working Paper 21865*. Retrieved from Stanford Center for Education Policy Analysis: http://cepa.stanford.edu/wp16–01.

Durlak, J. A., Domitrovich, C. E., Weissberg, R. P., & Gullotta, T. P. (Eds.). (2015). *Handbook of Social and Emotional Learning: Research and practice*. New York: The Guilford Press.

Erikson, E. H. (1968). *Identity: Youth and crisis*. New York: Norton.

Evans, N. J., Foreney, D. S., Guido, F. M., Patton, L. D. & Renn, K. A. (2010). *Student Development in College: Theory, research, and practice* (2nd ed.). San Francisco, CA: John Wiley & Sons.

Flum, H. & Kaplan, A. (2006). Exploratory orientation as an educational goal. *Educational Psychologist, 41*(2), 99–110.

French, S. E., Seidman, E., Allen, L. & Aber, J. L. (2006). The development of ethnic identity during adolescence. *Developmental Psychology, 42*(1), 1–10.

Friere, P. (1970). *Pedagogy of the Oppressed*. New York: The Seabury Press.

Hammond, Z. (2015). *Culturally Responsive Teaching and the Brain: Promoting authentic engagement and rigor among culturally and linguistically diverse students.* Thousand Oaks, CA: Corwin.

Hazen, E., Schlozman, S., & Beresin, E. (2008). Adolescent psychological development: A review. *Pediatrics in Review, 29*(5), 161–168.

hooks, b. (2015). Moving From Pain to Power: Choosing the space of radical openness. Scholar-in-Residence Program, Eugene Lang College of Liberal Arts, The New School, New York. Retrieved from www.youtube.com/watch?v=cpKuLl-GC0M.

Kohlberg, L. (1976). Moral Stages and Moralization. In T. Lickona (Ed.), *Moral development and behavior* (pp. 31–53). New York: Holt, Reinhart & Winston.

Marcia, J. E. (1993). The Relational Roots of Identity. In J. Kroger (Ed.), *Discussions on ego identity* (pp. 101–120). Hillsdale, NJ: Lawrence Erlbaum Associates.

Noam, G. (1999). The Psychology of Belonging: Reformulating adolescent development. In A. H. Esman, L. T. Flaherty, & H. A. Horowitz (Eds.), *Adolescent psychiatry: Annals of the American Society of Adolescent Psychiatry, 24* (pp. 49–68). Hillsdale, NJ: The Analytical Press.

Noam, G. & Fiore, N. (2004). Relationships across multiple settings: An overview. *New Directions for Youth Development, 103*, 9–16.

Phinney, J. S., Cantu, C. L. & Kurtz, D. A. (1997). Ethnic and American identity as predictors of self-esteem among African American, Latino, and White adolescents. *Journal of Youth and Adolescence, 26*(2), 165–185.

Phinney, J. S. & Ong, A. D. (2007). Conceptualization and measurement of ethnic identity: Current status and future directions. *Journal of Counseling Psychology, 54*(3), 271–281.

Schwartz, S. J., Zamboanga, B. L., Weisskirch, R. S., & Rodriguez, L. (2009). The relationships of personal and ethnic identity exploration to indices of adaptive and maladaptive psychosocial functioning. *International Journal of Behavioral Development, 33*(2), 131–144.

Shor, I. (1992). *Empowering Education: Critical teaching for social change.* Chicago, IL: The University of Chicago Press.

Siegel, D. (2013). *Brainstorm: The power and purpose of the teenage brain.* New York: Jeremy P. Tarcher/Penguin. (Kindle Version). Retrieved from Amazon.com

Steele, D. & Cohn-Vargas, B. (2013). *Identity Safe Classrooms: Places to belong and learn.* Thousand Oaks, CA: Corwin.

Steinberg, L. (2014). *Age of Opportunity: Lessons from the new science of adolescence.* New York: Houghton Mifflin Harcourt. (Kindle Version). Retrieved from Amazon.com.

Stroessner, S. & Good, C. (n.d.). *Stereotype Threat: An overview.* Retrieved from ReducingStereotypeThreat.org.

Swalwell, K. (2015). Mind the civic empowerment gap: Economically elite students and critical civic education. *Curriculum Inquiry, 45*(5), 491–512.

Tatum, B. D. (1992). Talking about race, learning about racism: The application of racial identity development theory in the classroom. *Harvard Educational Review, 62*(1), 1–24.

Toomey, R. & Umana-Taylor, A. (2012). The role of ethnic identity on self-esteem for ethnic minority youth: A brief review. *Prevention Researcher*, *19*(2), 8–12.

Torres, V. & Hernandez, E. (2007). The influence of ethnic identity on self-authorship: A longitudinal study of Latino/a college students. *Journal of College Student Development*, *48*(5), 558–573.

Umana-Taylor, A. J. & Updegraff, K. A. (2007). Latino adolescents' mental health: Exploring the interrelations among discrimination, ethnic identity, cultural orientation, self-esteem, and depressive symptoms. *Journal of Adolescence*, *30*, 549–567.

Willis, J. A. (2011). Nurturing students' brains for the future. *Learning Landscapes*, *5*(1), 259–265.

Wink, J. (2005). *Critical Pedagogy: Notes from the real world*. Boston, MA: Pearson Education.

Wortham, S. (2006). *Learning Identity: The joint emergence of social identification and academic learning*. New York: Cambridge University Press.

3

The Teacher's Role: Facilitating Dynamic Dialogues

Vicente doesn't think he's as smart as the other kids in the class, most of them white and middle class. He sees the papers they get back from teachers, and their grades are higher than his. He wishes school came easy for him like it does for Terrence or that he was naturally good in math like Marla. Terrance and Marla also attribute their success in school to their natural ability. What they don't know is that Vicente helps his mother clean office buildings at night, so he doesn't have much time to spend on homework. He's tired when he gets home, and on most nights, he doesn't feel like putting in a lot of effort. What Vicente doesn't know is that Terrance has a study area with a desk in his room, and Marla's father checks her math homework before she turns it in. Vicente's mother didn't finish high school, so she isn't much help with homework. And besides, she only speaks a little English. What Vicente also doesn't see about himself is that he has strengths that other students don't have. He is emotionally attuned and intuitive; his writing is heartfelt and visual; and his skill on the soccer field is impressive.

Transformational Inquiry (TI) relies on the unconditional premise that every student is lovable and capable of loving, and as such, every student is inherently brilliant and has a unique and important gift to offer the community. As students move through the personal, social, cognitive, and action domains of the TI process, they become more aware and accepting of their individual gifts and, likewise, more accepting and supportive of unique qualities in others. In a TI classroom, individuality and diversity flourish simultaneously. bell hooks (1994) sees love as the liberating force that inspires true learning. Siegel (2012; 2013) sees loving connections as the foundation of intelligent human development. Social emotional learning theory relies on the idea that students thrive in respectful relationships and contribute ethically to their peers, families, schools, and communities (Weissberg & Cascarino, 2013). Erikson (1968) and Kohlberg (1976) associate mature identity formation with integrity. Mozart quotes Nikolaus Joseph von Jacquin as saying, "True genius without heart is a thing of naught—for not great understanding alone, not intelligence alone, nor both together, make genius. Love! Love! Love! That is the soul of genius" (Solomon, 1966, p. 312). Love drives the TI method.

Because TI work is deeply personal, warmly welcoming students' emotional lives into the classroom is fundamental to the method. Emotional intensity is particularly prominent during adolescence, and processing uncomfortable feelings is a crucial part of exploration in identity formation. Many students, however, have learned to hide their emotions, directing attention away from uncomfortable feelings and distracting themselves instead. They grew up hearing messages that encouraged them to cut off from feelings rather than honor them: "Big girls don't cry," "Shake it off," and "Real men don't show feelings." By internalizing these messages, they learn to dismiss and deny their own feelings and, consequently, dismiss and deny the feelings of others. They have to counteract these tendencies to learn to pay attention to their feelings long enough to process them. Reflective practices can help them attune to their emotions by directing attention toward, rather than away from, feelings.

Grindon (2014) reminds us that "any heightened emotion leads to engagement, and student engagement is a significant predictor of achievement" (p. 265). As students become more comfortable with their feelings, their ability to handle cognitive dissonance increases. As they move through emotional resistance, they become more capable of thinking through complex problems. As their identities become stronger, they become less attached to the need for conventional approval, and thus become freer to think for themselves. They become more compassionate, but also develop the courage to be forthcoming about their inner truths. When students feel supported in a peer community, they become more likely to stand up to injustice. Learning to process emotions is crucial to emotional, social, intellectual, and ethical maturity.

> When students feel supported in a peer community, they become more likely to stand up to injustice.

The Teacher's Role

Individuals drawn to the teaching profession are typically self-aware, socially attuned, and caring, as these qualities underlie good teaching in general. Most teachers read the room constantly to gauge interest and enthusiasm for learning. They know how to engage students and facilitate participation in discussions. They check in with individual students if they perceive problems or conflicts. Teachers notice body language, facial expressions, or a shift in the quality of a student's response in class. If something seems off, intuitive teachers do not hesitate to ask questions, and students are almost always glad they noticed and cared enough to inquire. Because conversations about identity can be sensitive, the most important qualities a teacher can have are empathy and a keen ear for listening. Teachers need not try to "fix" their students. If classroom conversations bring up discomfort or pain, trust that students are capable, through a reliable process of inquiry and personal reflection, to process their discomfort. By witnessing this model at work over time, teachers learn to trust the process.

The teacher's role is to manage boundaries in discussions, maintain adherence to discussion guidelines, and create a safe environment in which students find meaning and purpose in sharing their stories with each other. Bringing their stories to the forefront of the curriculum makes learning come alive for them. Linda Christensen (2009) says, "Putting students' lives at the center of the curriculum tells them they matter—their lives, their ancestors' lives are important" (p. 4). She reminds us that learning does not take place in isolation from the world, but in interaction with it. In a world in which sensitive conversations are typically avoided, students appreciate being able to speak openly with each other. They find conflict resolution to be challenging, yet honorable, work, and the greater intimacy and authenticity that result are tremendously rewarding. They thrive in a supportive learning community.

> In a world in which sensitive conversations are typically avoided, students appreciate being able to speak openly with each other.

Establishing a safe learning community requires a strong code of ethics when conversations involve students' identities. Teachers need to be prepared to help them negotiate this sometimes unfamiliar and unexamined social-emotional terrain. TI begins with creating a space of belonging where students can self-reveal without risk of judgment. When the need to belong is met, students are freer to develop cognitively because much of the fear that consumes their attention is alleviated. When students have a safe place to process feelings, they often achieve important insights into their personal dilemmas.

Their attention is freed to focus on higher order learning: emotionally, cognitively, and morally. Out of this process, higher order human qualities invariably emerge: respect, empathy, honesty, trust, acceptance, and unity.

Seven Principles of Transformational Inquiry

TI relies on acknowledging and validating students' emotional lives, facilitating supportive social relationships, connecting their deeper feelings to avenues for cognitive growth, and testing their knowledge in real-world action. Welcoming the emotional lives of adolescents into the classroom, however, is not for the faint of heart. It takes courage, patience, compassion, willingness to make mistakes, and persistence to master the facilitation process. Managing classroom dynamics requires socially savvy and highly developed communication skills. Connecting the students' interests and experience to academic learning and providing frameworks for action demands flexibility. Yet, the rewards are enormous for both students and teachers.

The following guidelines can help teachers respond to the discussions that emerge from important and meaningful identity-based themes. The teacher's work is to create an inclusive learning environment and guide students as they move toward greater empathy, understanding, and insight.

1. *Every Story is a Love Story*

Every human being wants nothing more than to be loved and accepted by others. If followed to its emotional roots, there is a desire for love at the heart of every story. Whether it be love for others or self-love grounded in integrity Gilligan and Brown's landmark longitudinal studies (1998) outline the tension many young adolescent girls feel as they strive to shape themselves to fit social norms in their quest to belong, often to their psychological detriment. Rather than expressing the truth of their inner experience, many girls pretend to be what they believe will win them social acceptance. Their integrity gets pushed underground as they begin to search for an identity outside themselves: in media images, in popularity, in trying to win the approval of boys, in always being "nice." The resulting mismatch between affect and behavior may create an inner disconnect that compromises a sense of integrity which is so essential to self-esteem, healthy relationships, and identity formation. Girls caught in this dynamic often have difficulty forming genuine friendships because hey hide their authentic feelings under a cloud of pretense, opting instead for superficial relationships based on fear and power. Because it is socially unacceptable for girls to express feelings of hurt and anger directly, they get power through gossip and other forms of relational aggression (Caldwell & Swift, 2003). Whereas Gilligan and Brown applied this dynamic to adolescent girls, we see it at work to varying degrees in the development of all social identities, particularly among adolescents.

Conversations in which students share their internal experience, including the pain of trying to conform to negative stereotypes, can help them learn to share the parts of themselves they keep hidden and learn to address conflict directly and authentically. The supportive bonds they form in the process give them a sense of belonging in a peer group based on respect, acceptance, and a commitment to their own development. They gain a sense of their own identity based in authenticity and integrity. Supplemental academic materials on identity development help solidify their social emotional gains.

> Conversations in which students share their internal experience, including the pain of trying to conform to negative stereotypes, can help adolescents learn to share the parts of themselves they keep hidden . . .

Learning to love and respect one's self is an important component of overcoming internalized oppression, and seeing one's self mirrored and supported by others is a necessary part of this process. Empathetic mirroring shifts self-perception and reinforces positive identity. Siegel (2013) explains that relationships "in which you feel felt by another person—when you sense that your internal world, your mind, is taken in by another and respected—are the building blocks of health" (p. 215).

2. Listening is Enough

Teachers who understand the power of compassionate listening know that listening is enough. The act of listening attentively to students' stories without feeling the need to "fix" them or any aspects of their lives is a powerful teaching gift and honors our students' capacity to process their own experience, solve their own problems, and think for themselves. In the vast majority of cases, students are equipped to handle the issues they face in their lives, and the simple act of validating a student's experience is all that is required of the teacher (and peers). While every life is fraught with struggle, almost all students have the strength to meet the challenges they face. In cases in which a student may not have the inner resources to face common human dilemmas, or if the issues they face lie outside the boundaries of normal development, they should be referred to a school counselor for further guidance.

Teachers model the art of empathetic listening and offer clear guidelines to students. Students learn to listen with 100 percent of their attention, with an attitude of acceptance, respect, and with an open mind. Body language is important. Side conversations or comments, eye rolling, "exchanging a look" with a friend, or laughing while someone is sharing are disrespectful behaviors that thwart the goals of a safe learning community. Students learn to respond to other students with compassionate, supportive, and honest feedback. They learn to be present, attune to the other person's inner experience, and hear the story as the speaker's experiential truth. They are coached to be mindful of comments or questions that could undermine the speaker's sense of trust in them as listeners.

Students are also instructed on how to share time equitably, and this guideline applies to the teacher, as well. The teacher's role is to facilitate and guide discussions among students, and while teachers can certainly participate in the discussions, they should be careful not to dominate.

3. *The Personal is Universal*

Enormous power lies in the courage to share one's self authentically. As teachers, we understand the importance of being truly known in order to form connections with others. For most of our students, however, this may not be so apparent, and they need encouragement to reveal the deeper parts of themselves to each other. As we witness our students' journeys of discovery, we see them make the transition from the egocentric consciousness of childhood (in which they see themselves as the center of the universe) to a more flexible identity that can view life from multiple perspectives. During adolescence, identity may shift dramatically between egocentric and multiple perspectives as young people learn to negotiate the shifting terrain between self and others.

> . . . identity may shift dramatically between egocentric and multiple perspectives as young people learn to negotiate the shifting terrain between self and others.

Adolescents are in the process of learning to see themselves as others see them, which can be a painful process at times. When the focal point of their identity suddenly shifts to the outside, they find themselves in the uncomfortable position of relying on others to show them who they are. As Gilligan and Brown's (1998) research emphasizes, young people frequently respond by attempting to shape themselves into what they believe others will find acceptable. They conform to others' expectations in an attempt to fit in. Yet in the very act of trying to gain acceptance, adolescents often thwart acceptance by wearing a mask that covers their authentic thoughts, feelings, attitudes, and ideas. They hide their unique qualities (lest they be thought "weird"), keep their opinions quiet for fear of offending someone, hide their insecurities, and pretend they have their act together. In short, they strive to be like everyone else rather than asserting their individual differences. Paradoxically, they feel that in order to be allowed into relationships, they have to keep large parts of themselves out of relationships. Unfortunately, the parts of themselves they hide—their unique selves—are crucial to forming authentic relationships. What is the value of being accepted if you have to pretend you are someone you are not?

Students find that when they share personal stories, others relate strongly. Stories about being bullied (or bullying), jockeying for a higher position in the popularity matrix, dealing with the wrath of an older sibling, conflict with parents, struggling in math class, self-consciousness about appearance, and a host of other typical adolescent insecurities (often based on internalized oppression) are common human dilemmas. They realize their stories inspire empathy and understanding in others, and rather than alienate them, sharing their deeper thoughts and feelings brings them closer.

4. Feelings Are the Beginning of Insight

Students enter our classroom with a host of unexamined assumptions about their own identities and those of others. Girls, for instance, sometimes believe that sexual harassment is "normal" and just part of life. When they hear their experience echoed in each other's stories, they begin to see sexism as a social construct. Heightened awareness of systemic injustice may cause feelings to initially intensify. Confusion, anger, sadness, and guilt are common, even healthy, responses to ill-treatment.

Sometimes, students are moved to tears, and when they are, teachers simply model empathetic listening. They need not try to stop the tears, but instead reassure students that their feelings are respected. There is no need to intervene or fix, but only to bear witness and hold space for emotional expression.

After an emotional story is shared, asking the question "How did you feel hearing this?" gives other students an opportunity to offer feedback. Invariably, they say they feel honored to be present. They express respect and admiration. Empathetic feedback reassures students who courageously express their emotions that they have moved closer to their peers rather than alienated themselves.

It is important for teachers of all races to protect students of color when they are sharing experiences of race discrimination. Likewise, teachers of every gender should protect students who share stories of gender discrimination. A student who invalidates someone else's story is almost always attempting to avoid his or her own feelings. Because some students feel safer debating issues than revealing feelings, they may attempt to steer the conversation away from the emotional realm and shift the discussion to the intellectual realm. Careful facilitation keeps students' attention on respecting each other's *felt experience*. If the conversation turns into a debate, the process has gone awry, and students should be redirected to attune to their feelings.

Teachers can gently address and redirect comments that minimize, rationalize, or contradict another student's feelings or experience. Writing a response outside of class about feelings that arose while hearing the story can help these students process what is likely guilt or denial. Privileged students, especially, are sometimes uncomfortable hearing about the struggles of devalued groups because they feel "guilt by association." *It is important not to let the student of privilege become the focus of the group process.* When students make themselves vulnerable by sharing stories of discrimination, it is important to keep the focus on those students so they do not leave the classroom feeling exposed or invalidated. Shifting the focus of attention to the person of privilege can undermine the healing process for both students.

5. We Are All Part of a Larger Human Family

In spite of our differences, we bear many commonalities. Chief among our commonalities is that we all share a common human identity. Siegel (2013) believes that many of the world's problems could be addressed by expanding our identities beyond the concept of a separate self:

> When we see ourselves as separate, we are not facing the reality of our interdependent, interconnected nature. We are not integrating our identity with the larger world that we are fundamentally a part of. It just may be that many of our biggest challenges are in fact revealed as the chaos and rigidity of such impaired integration, a state created by our human sense of a separate self that assumes happiness comes from material acquisitions alone and that infinite consumption is possible on our resource-limited planet.
>
> (p. 303)

Identity development involves a process of individuation in which students define themselves according to characteristics that make them unique, but also according to what they have in common with others. Individuation and diversity, cultural and otherwise, are intricately linked and rely on each other for higher orders of development. When students see their experience mirrored in the eyes of their peers, it helps them accept their own unique characteristics. When they hear each other's stories, they learn to mirror, reflect, and empathize. They also come to realize they are not so different after all. At the same time, they realize that socially constructed differences are important aspects of identity because these differences convey or limit political power and have material effects on certain bodies.

Ultimately, what they discover is that the higher order social emotional values they generated in the beginning of the course to make their learning community safe are the same values that make it possible to transcend cultural differences and transform their relationships. These values include empathy, authenticity, acceptance, compassion, justice, and love. They also realize that the dehumanization of the other lies at the heart of oppression, and overcoming oppression involves reconnecting to these re-humanaizing values.

6. Perfection is the Enemy of Intimacy

Adolescents, like many adults, sometimes fail to realize that it is more important to be human than to appear perfect. Perfectionism thwarts authenticity. It causes people to confuse vulnerability with weakness and hide behind pretenses. Our imperfections connect us to each other as part of the human condition, which requires that we respond to each other's pain with compassion, as well as share in each other's joy.

Students need encouragement to be willing to make mistakes. Learning begins when one becomes aware of what one does not know. Feeling stupid and/or wrong can be extremely uncomfortable, and yet when the embarrassment is processed, it quickly evolves into humor. Nonetheless, exposing oneself as ignorant can be a huge risk in any situation, but especially in a class in which sensitive subjects are addressed. White students, in particular, are reluctant to talk about race because they are afraid of saying "the wrong thing." When a student inadvertently says something insensitive, a gentle correction or redirection is usually enough. Students almost always want to be compassionate, and much can be gained by assuming good will.

> Students need encouragement to be willing to make mistakes. Learning begins when one becomes aware of what one does not know.

7. Conflict can be Productive

Conflict is an essential component of real-life learning. A classroom can act as a container for conflict to be resolved through a precise and reliable process. Students learn to "lean into the discomfort" and find their "learning edge." They learn to recognize conflict as part of a productive part of learning.

Gorski (2009) describes cognitive dissonance as "when a learner—any one of us—finds her- or himself grappling with new information in light of old understandings." When a student encounters information that contradicts a preexisting assumption, she may respond defensively, not wanting to take in the new information, and she may grapple with the difference between what she thought she knew and the new information. Gorski sees cognitive dissonance as a fundamental component of learning and recommends teaching students about it explicitly. He says, "I have come to learn that these moments form the critical crossroads of learning, the educational moments of truth, in my social justice teaching" (p. 54).

James and Davidson (2005) emphasize that conflict can be used as a catalyst to enhance relationships when individuals learn how to use it. They relate "high-quality, energizing relationships across difference" to a learning mindset in which individuals are truly curious about their differences. These types of relationships can be created through the development of perspective taking, empathy; a strong feedback process that includes self-disclosure; and listening skills.

Working through conflict is an important aspect of the TI method, but it can take time and sometimes more than one class period. Letting students know from the beginning that conflict may arise, providing instruction in conflict resolution skills, and encouraging them to stick with the process helps them through conflict.

Including Parents

Because TI taps into the emotional realm of personal and social identity, it is especially important for teachers to be grounded in pedagogical theory and best practices. Administrators, colleagues, students, and parents need to understand the value of the method and be able to defend it against criticism, if necessary.

Communication with parents is an important part of the TI method, and when teachers model aspects of the method in their relationships with parents, supportive relationships are the norm. We communicate early in the year with parents through an email that outlines the goals of the class. We briefly position the TI method in educational tradition, theory, and research. We let them know we want to work alongside them to facilitate a healthy identity in their child. We invite them to engage with us in the process of teaching by having frequent discussions about the material from the class at home, reading articles along with us, contributing sources, and inviting guest speakers.

Finally, we stress the importance of parents and teachers being on the same team and encourage them to contact us if they have concerns.

TI curriculum includes activities for students to share with their parents, such as parent interviews about values, experiences with discrimination, and discussions about religious beliefs. Parents appreciate that their children are engaged, motivated, and at an age when withdrawal from parents is considered common, their child is talking to them about meaningful learning in school.

Conclusion

TI capitalizes on students' interests and addresses key developmental needs. Bringing personal narratives into the classroom connects their lives outside of school to work in the classroom and makes learning meaningful. Learning authentic communication skills facilitates positive and supportive relationships, which fosters learning gains. Through listening to their own voices and the voices of others, students' identities are strengthened and academic confidence increases.

Processing feelings is the beginning of insight but not the end. Student stories provide springboards for making connections to the larger world they live in, and studies in histories, politics, literature, and other academic disciplines consolidate insights and expand worldviews. Scaffolding personal, social, cognitive, and action-oriented activities helps students learn systematic thinking and self-directed learning. Guided by their own questions, which arise out of their personal and social experiences, students become inspired to pursue rigorous academic work.

References

Caldwell, M. & Swift, J. (2003). Beyond "mean girl" typecasting: Power, popularity and potential. *Schoolbook: A Journal of Education, 12*(2), 3–8.

Christensen, L. (2009). *Teaching for Joy and Justice*. Milwaukee, WI: Rethinking Schools.

Erikson, E. H. (1968). *Identity: Youth and crisis*. New York: Norton.

Gilligan, C. & Brown, L. M. (1998). *Meeting at the Crossroads: Women's psychology and girls' development*. New York: Ballentine Books.

Gorski, P. (2009). Cognitive dissonance as a strategy in social justice teaching. *Multicultural Education, 17*(1), 54–57.

Grindon, K. (2014). Advocacy at the core: Inquiry and empowerment in the time of the common core state standards. *Language Arts, 91*(4), 251–266.

hooks, b. (1994). *Teaching to Transgress: Education as the practice of freedom*. New York: Routledge.

James, E. H. & Davidson, M. N. (2005). The engines of positive relationships across difference: Learning and conflict. Working Paper Series, paper no. 05–11. Retrieved from www.academia.edu/641672/The_engines_of_positive_relationships_across_difference_Conflict_and_learning.

Kohlberg, L. (1976). Moral Stages and Moralization. In T. Lickona (Ed.), *Moral development and behavior* (pp. 31–53). New York: Holt, Reinhart, and Winston.

Siegel, D. (2012). The brain and the developing mind. Chautauqua Institute. Retrieved from http://library.fora.tv/2009/06/30/Dan_Siegel_The_Brain_and_the_Developing_Mind.

Siegel, D. (2013). *Brainstorm: The power and purpose of the Teenage Brain*. New York: Jeremy P. Tarcher/Penguin. (Kindle Version). Retrieved from Amazon.com.

Solomon, M. (1966). *Mozart: A life*. New York: Harper Perennial.

Weissberg, R. P. & Cascarino, J. (2013, Oct). Academic learning + social emotional learning = national priority. *Kappan Magazine, 95*(2), 8–13.

4

Inquiry Into Identity:
Introductory Explorations

Brian, a bright yet underachieving student, identifies as white. He rarely takes assignments seriously, has difficulty focusing, and frequently doesn't turn in homework. He prefers playing video games or goofing off with his friends in his spare time. He frustrates teachers because he has enormous potential as a student, yet his potential remains largely unrealized. In his "Family History Project" presentation, Brain shares that his mother is Native American and grew up on a reservation. He shows photographs of her family and tells stories about ancestors who fled into the woods to avoid Removal and of living relatives who have faced racism. Later in the semester, Brian researches the history of his mother's tribe/community for his "People's Histories Project "and identifies how his family's stories fit into the historical timeline. His presentation is organized, thorough, well documented, and personal. Brian brings fry bread to share with the class. His classmates, riveted by the information he shares with them, see a side of Brian they have not seen before. Brian, too, sees himself in a new way. In connecting to his Native roots, he feels pride in his history, and at the same time, systems of discrimination become relevant for him. He is motivated to learn more because he has discovered something worth knowing. Suddenly, learning becomes meaningful and school has purpose. His grades improve, not only in our class, but in other classes as well.

Transformational Inquiry (TI) provides a template for students to move from self-discovery to self-revelation to self-advocacy to self-determination.

The introductory unit launches this process. As students explore each stage of the process, they integrate information from the personal, social, cognitive, and action domains of learning. They engage in activities to inspire them to reflect inwardly, to share their experience with each other, to make cognitive connections to extend their insights, and finally, to take action on what they have learned. Many students thrive in the personal and social domain, while others feel more comfortable in the cognitive domain. Either way, the connections they make between domains strengthen learning (Pelligrino & Hilton, 2012).

The lessons in the introductory unit can be used in any humanities course as an introductory or tertiary unit, or as an ongoing component interspersed throughout the curriculum. These lessons have been used in advisory curricula in middle schools; high school teachers have used aspects of them in biology, math, history, and literature classes; and coaches have used them for team building. We encourage teachers to adapt these lessons to their students' needs and use them in part or in whole to complement their existing curricula and to augment their teaching passions. These lessons, like all TI lessons, reflect the Common Core State Standards (CCSS) because they share the key objective: facilitating higher order thinking. The lessons also relate to a variety of skills emphasized in the CCSS Language Arts and Social Studies standards for instruction. In the context of identity explorations, the lessons teach proficiency in reading; identifying main ideas; summarizing, interpreting, and analyzing meaning in texts; identifying bias; and synthesizing information from multiple sources. They particularly emphasize the CCSS Language Arts standards for instruction to facilitate speaking and listening skills; and link to many states' standards for social emotional learning.

These lessons lay important groundwork for conversations about identity, which will occur in greater depth in the units on race, gender, and social class. Before productive communication about these sensitive subjects can occur, students need to master a set of social emotional skills to establish identity safety: how to self-reflect, how to listen without judgment, and how to express respect and appreciation for others. Teachers introduce the concept that learning itself is an emotional and social process and that learning occurs in community. Because transformational learning is unlike the content-based learning to which most students are accustomed, they must also question and redefine what learning means to them.

In *Identity Safe Classrooms*, Steele and Cohn-Vargas (2013) emphasize the importance of teachers knowing their students as individuals. While students are psychologically and materially affected by their social identities, they are nonetheless unique individuals and need to be recognized as such. In *Everyday*

Antiracism, Pollack (2008, p. 64) likewise affirms, "There is no shortcut to coming to know the student as an individual." In a TI classroom, students are the primary source for their own identities. The teacher's role is to "listen for student voices" (Steele & Cohn-Vargas, p. 23) and help them articulate their feelings, thoughts, and ideas. Teachers give up the "all knowing adult role" (Pollack, 2008, p. 36), as they become activators and facilitators of learning. They learn alongside their students.

TI teachers share as much power as possible with students. They facilitate student leadership and encourage initiative for learning and managing the class. Students generate rules, contribute articles, choose research topics, choose literature books, and submit news stories. They teach each other through collaborative learning projects and presenting information. They give each other feedback and assess each other's projects. They evaluate themselves at the end of the semester.

Introducing the Transformational Inquiry Practice

The introductory unit lays the groundwork for students to explore their identities in the personal, social, cognitive, and action domains. It introduces the method for establishing an identity-safe learning community, offering students both theory and practice exercises for self-attunement and activities to facilitate identifying and expressing emotions. Because learning and identity are so intimately connected, these lessons provide reflection on individual learning styles, as well as cultural ways of knowing. The concepts of cognitive dissonance and "learning edge" are introduced, so students can learn to monitor internal tension to maximize learning. A set of scenarios helps them identify how learning is commonly undermined and develop strategies to interrupt unhealthy classroom dynamics. Students are introduced to identity formation theory, and they begin exploring their social identities. They learn fundamental concepts of oppression theory through an interactive exercise using an identity they all share, that of a teenager. Finally, they explore their family histories and make presentations in class.

Setting the Stage for Transformational Inquiry

When students understand how they can expect to benefit from a class, what the teacher expects from them, and how they will be assessed, they feel a sense of security and belonging (Steele & Cohn-Vargas, 2013). Teachers accomplish these goals by introducing the purpose of the course, setting high expectations, and involving students in the work of establishing an identity-safe classroom in the first lesson. Providing an assessment rubric lets students know how they will be evaluated and prepares them for the noncognitive dimensions of the class. Lesson 4.1, *Setting the Stage for Inquiry Into Identity* (page 66), provides an assessment rubric, a student handout outlining expectations, and a questionnaire to guide their reflections on what they need from the class to feel safe.

Creating an Identity-Safe Classroom

Establishing clear guidelines for supportive communication is the first order of business because the work of identity formation depends on a secure environment. In Lesson 4.2, *Creating an Identity-Safe Learning Community* (page 70), teachers lay the groundwork for the important work to come. The question "What do you need from the people in this room to feel safe enough to talk about your authentic feelings?" generates guidelines that set the tone for the rest of the year. The answers this question elicits rarely vary, no matter the age or demographics of the group. Different groups of students generate similar criteria for safety: respect, empathy, honesty, courage, confidentiality, trust, acceptance, and, of course, the right to privacy. Apparently, any group, no matter their age, race, gender, social class, or religion, needs these higher order social emotional qualities to safely share their deeper truths in a community. These qualities transcend individual experiences and diverse identities to create a framework in which social identities can be safely explored. When students have completed the "What Do You Need to Feel Safe" questionnaire in Lesson 4.1, they are primed for this discussion.

After generating the list, the students commit to building a learning community with these qualities at the foundation. Because they have generated the guidelines themselves, they take them seriously and use them to keep each other honest during discussions. When students themselves make the rules, teachers rarely have to enforce them. Students instead take ownership of the room. Some teachers follow up by asking students to synthesize information from the first two lessons to create a class contract, or guiding document, that can be invoked throughout the year to remind students of their agreement. Such documents are powerful instruments when generated by students.

Young people are hungry for a community in which they can reveal themselves and be accepted for "just being who they are." They want nothing more than to be heard and understood. They are eager to make authentic connections and only need to be shown how. As the personal and social inquiries proceed, students need encouragement to be honest, to say what they think, how they feel, and share what they find meaningful. Honesty and authenticity are contagious, and when a few students lead the way, others follow. Once the boundaries are established, they begin right away. To reinforce safety, the student handout "Creating an Identity-Safe Learning Community" introduces important communication skills such as active listening, sharing time fairly, giving respectful feedback, and asking open-ended questions.

> Young people are hungry for a community in which they can reveal themselves and be accepted for "just being who they are." They want nothing more than to be heard and understood.

After reviewing the guidelines, students can practice listening and sharing skills in pairs. In this activity, one student adopts the role of listener while the other takes the role of sharer. If students need a prompt, the question "What's going on in your life right now?" should suffice. After five minutes, they switch roles. When they have each had a turn at listening and sharing, they return to the large group to report on their experience. They talk about what it felt like to listen with full attention, what it felt like to share without interruption, and the emotions they witnessed, as well as the ones they experienced. They can also talk about what they learned about themselves, about someone else, or about the general process of listening and sharing. Writing a half-page summary about their experiences helps them develop and refine their thoughts, consolidating their insight from the experiences in the day and the whole class discussion. Students love sharing information with each other in these dyads. They usually ask to do the exercise again. This exercise can be repeated throughout the year, with different partners and with longer periods of time for listening and sharing.

Inquiry Into Emotions

Many people, perhaps especially those in academia, believe the intellectual domain is superior to the emotional domain. This internalized hierarchy sets the stage for "privileged knowledge" or knowledge constructed by dominant social groups. Kumashiro (2012) discusses long-standing critiques that the structure and curriculum of schooling privileges a particular racial consciousness (white), a particular gender consciousness (male), and a particular class consciousness (middle to upper). Privileged knowledge excludes the knowledge of power-out social groups, which may be intuitive or feeling-based. The experience of having what one knows excluded is in itself emotional. Thus, the hierarchical assumption that the intellect is superior to the emotions must be interrogated in a TI classroom. TI seeks to provide a balance between the intellectual and affective domains, recognizing the importance of the so-called "masculine" abilities (analytical thinking and writing), but also emphasizing "feminine" abilities (emotional honesty; speaking and writing from the heart) as equally important.

Some students, particularly if they come from white middle-class backgrounds, have been conditioned to repress, deny, or hide strong emotions. These students need instruction in how to self-attune and counteract emotional avoidance to get the most out of learning. When emotions are welcomed as an essential component of the learning process, affective data can be integrated with cognitive processing to make learning not only meaningful, but also rewarding and fun. Students who are learning to synthesize information from a variety of sources should realize that their own emotions are an invaluable source of data. As a result of emotional engagement, they become highly motivated to learn.

In Lesson 4.3, *Understanding Emotions as Power* (page 72), students complete a questionnaire in which they examine their relationship with feelings. They reflect on their internal experience and then share with others in the class. Students identify common patterns of emotional expression and resistance among them. They readily identify themselves within these patterns and recognize that the patterns among them reflect larger social and cultural patterns.

It is important for teachers to convey that the goal is not merely to express emotions, but to *process* emotions to gain the benefit of objectivity. Students should also understand that some emotions must be processed slowly over a period of time. The discussion of what kinds of emotions are difficult for students to process can be helpful to the teacher as the year progresses. When students identify the kinds of feelings they find difficult to attend to, the teacher can gently coach them in how to process those feelings should they arise.

> **It is important for teachers to convey that the goal is not merely to express emotions, but to *process* emotions to gain the benefit of objectivity.**

Inquiry Into Learning

Essential questions lay the groundwork for inquiry learning used throughout the course. Such questions arise from genuine curiosity and reflect what students really want to know. Essential questions motivate students to acquire content knowledge, but more importantly, they connect them to their desire to learn. McTighe and Wiggins (2013, pp. 17–18) describe the power of essential questions:

> As the child in "The Emperor's New Clothes," Pooh in "Winnie the Pooh," and Socrates in *Plato's Dialogues* remind us, to persist in asking questions when others don't is the key to escaping the bounds of unthinking habit, belief and dogma. Once we have learned to question—really question—then we are immunized from falling victim to people who want us not to think too hard about what they say, be it politicians, advertisers or bullying associates.

Voicing essential questions deepens, enriches, and makes public the desire for knowledge.

Teachers can pose essential questions when introducing key concepts. The question "What do you already know?" gives teachers insight into students' background knowledge. "What do you want to learn?" can guide inquiry studies. Essential questions can also be assigned in response to readings. For instance, when students read Jones's (2000) "Levels of Racism: A Theoretic Framework and a Gardener's Tale," an article about white privilege, they list the authentic questions that arise in their minds in response to this thought-provoking article.

Learning Identity

Given that (1) identity and learning are intricately related, (2) racist and sexist stereotypes denigrate the intelligence of students of color and women and girls, (3) the effects of stereotype threat are well documented, (4) students who struggle with attention and learning issues frequently lose academic confidence, and (5) a significant number of students have adopted an anti-intellectual stance regarding school, questioning the nature of learning is an important aspect of TI. The question "What is learning?" begins a provocative discussion. Inquiries into learning guide students to think about learning in new ways. Students share stories of repressing, rather than voicing, questions for fear of being ridiculed, pretending to know the answer because they are afraid to look stupid, and pretending *not* to know the answer because they are afraid of being seen as "too smart." Kiran, a student with ADHD, writes that he became aware of his learning issues in fifth grade. "I was not very good at paying attention in class and I was having trouble writing essays. That's when I realized I was different from others because of my performance." By the time he got to seventh grade, he had lost interest in school. "I disliked being there. I felt like I was being put in a box." Later in the year, he redefined his learning style as creative and said, "I may still struggle in school but that doesn't mean I'm not smart."

These discussions help students understand how social dynamics and insecurities about intelligence affect interest in and learning in school. When they reflect on and discuss their experience, anti-intellectual cultural patterns become visible to them. Subsequently, when they notice themselves shrinking away from full participation in learning, they can take action to counteract these tendencies.

Cognitive Dissonance

The concept of cognitive dissonance plays a key role in the TI method. Because students discuss sensitive subjects, we want them to understand that learning, at its best, can sometimes be uncomfortable, and yet they nonetheless need to take appropriate risks in discussions to achieve genuine interaction. The more comfortable they become with cognitive dissonance, the more expansive their identities become and the more sophisticated their thinking. They need to understand that resistance to believing their classmates' experiences can be a defense against guilt by association. Over time, as they process their feelings, they became more capable of understanding the role oppression plays in the lives of other people, as well as the role cognitive dissonance plays in their own thinking and learning.

The Power of Mirroring

Individuation and diversity are intricately linked and flourish simultaneously in a TI classroom. Siegel (2013, p. 170) emphasizes that healthy relationships both "honor differences and promote linkage." Identity is relational, and subjectivity of the self is formed through interactions with others. It is through healthy relationships that students grow and develop.

Adolescents are shifting their locus of awareness to the outside in an effort to glean what others think of them (Caldwell & Swift, 2003). They may be insecure about their position in the social hierarchy and are paying close attention to how to advance their standing. They often try to shape themselves to fit their idea of what will win the approval of peers: the right clothes, the right attitude, the right language, and the right associates. They are keenly aware of who says hello to them and who doesn't, who sits with them at lunch, and who "likes" their posts on social media. If they are alone rather than with friends during a break or between classes, they worry they may be perceived as a social pariah.

The mechanisms of popularity and social jockeying, closely associated with the phenomenon of bullying, are largely driven by social insecurity and the lack of a strong personal identity grounded in integrity. Because so much of bullying targets students' social identities, these stories often emerge in the classroom. Students share stories in which they have been victimized, witnessed, been afraid to stand up to bullying or bullied others. Almost every student has a story about trying to become more popular. They tell stories of betraying friends who aren't "cool" and stories of being betrayed because they weren't "cool" enough. Sometimes the events in these stories happened years earlier, yet when students share them, the pain is still as fresh as when the incident happened.

> Adolescents' interest in their social standing consumes a tremendous amount of their attention, and opening these issues up for such discussions in the classroom taps into a wellspring of emotional and mental energy that can be transmuted into motivation for learning.

Adolescents' interest in their social standing consumes a tremendous amount of their attention, and opening these issues up for such discussions in the classroom taps into a wellspring of emotional and mental energy that can be transmuted into motivation for learning. Through examining their own experience, feelings, and attitudes about their position in the social hierarchy at school, students can connect what they already know to how power and privilege operate in institutions like schools, religions, governments, and businesses when they study race, gender, and social class.

Social Identity

Lesson 4.4, *What is Your Social Identity?* (page 74) stimulates reflection about personal identity and gives students a chance to talk to each other about important aspects of their social identities. Identity does not always fit neatly into boxes on a grid, so students may grapple with how to complete the matrix. Some students do not identify with a particular race or ethnicity; religious affiliation may not be an important part of their lives; or their sexual identity may be open to question.

The "Social Identity Matrix" activity reveals concepts that were not previously apparent. First, social identities are not necessarily visible, so students get to know each other better as individuals. Second, it becomes obvious that different identity groups weigh the importance to their social identities differently. For instance, whites typically assign little importance to their racial identity (perhaps a 2 or 3), while students of color usually assign greater importance to their race (8 or 9). Girls generally give their gender identity far more weight than boys do. Jewish and Muslim students give religious identity more weight than Christians. The more disempowered an identity, the more important it becomes in the mind of the individual. Such identities carry more mental weight because they require conscious attention to defend against discrimination. The dual consciousness Dubois described over a hundred years ago (Dubois, 1897) is still very much a factor in the minds of students of color and other marginalized groups. These aspects of their identities take on heightened importance, in part, because they have to be aware of the "other" to protect against the real possibility that they may be misjudged or stereotyped. Others may also remind them they are different. As Sierra, an African American student, wrote, "I'd just like to go through one day without being reminded of my race."

Asking students to theorize possible (or actual) reasons for this phenomenon stimulates their thinking and allows them to postulate rationales for what they have observed. They may also offer other categories of identity not listed on the grid. Students may have particular talents that make up a significant part of their identities. For instance, Ingrid defined herself as smart, Daniel considered himself an artist, Craig was an expert at the video game Super Mario Brothers, Michael was good at soccer, and Nick was an accomplished violinist. Including categories of talent or achievement reveals positive aspects of identity that can counteract the negative effects of marginalized social identities.

Power and Politics in the Classroom and Beyond

Exploring social identities leads into discussions of power and privilege. The concept of privilege can be difficult for students in a dominant group to grasp, and understanding comes gradually. White students, for instance, may not see immediately that they have social privilege based on their race. They are unaccustomed to thinking about their race because they have the privilege of not having to. Unlike students of color, they rarely need to be aware of other people's potentially racialized perceptions of them. Students of color, however, understand the concept of privilege immediately because they experience the dual consciousness of "watching themselves being watched." They have learned to see themselves through the eyes of a white supremacist mindset in order to defend themselves against racism. Likewise, young men do not necessarily understand male privilege. They may initially resist accepting that young women are affected by gender stereotypes that diminish their self-worth. As students hear their classmates' stories and connect them to academic materials, they become more open to understanding the concept of privilege.

Oppression and Resistance

Finally, before embarking onto the units on race, gender, and class, students need to understand the concepts of oppression and resistance. These terms are introduced in an exercise designed to elucidate the effects of stereotypes (see iChange collaborative website (2016) for lesson plan). The "What's Great/ What's Not" activity can be done using any social identity, but in the introductory unit, we use an identity all students share, that of a teenager. Students respond to the question "What's great about being a teenager?" They brainstorm a list of things they like about being a teenager, listing such things as having more responsibility and trust from their parents, being able to go to movies with more adult ratings, learning to drive, having more privileges than their younger siblings, being able to stay up late, and being able to hang out with their friends. After students have exhausted all the positive aspects of being a teenager, the teacher flips the discussion and asks, "What is difficult about being a teenager?" They list common stereotypes about teenagers: always seen as moody, erratic and hormonal; selfish, rebellious or rude; not taken seriously by adults; excluded from important conversations; feeling awkward; and not being trusted by parents.

The second list "What's Not" characterizes "oppression" because it shows how teenagers are frequently devalued in society. Students *feel* these stereotypes; they believe they are unfair and do not accurately characterize them. Teachers can emphasize that, indeed, that is how oppression feels. Students readily transfer the "oppression" of being a teenager to that of other social identities (race, gender, social class, etc.), in which similar patterns of unfairness occur. This activity opens the door to understanding the language of oppression and resistance used throughout the course.

We distinguish between four kinds of oppression: institutional, intergroup, internalized, and personally mitigated. *Institutional* (or systemic) oppression operates through laws, policies, or beliefs. It is manifested in government, social, or religious institutions. Jim Crow laws, the glass ceiling, and religions that do not allow women in leadership roles exemplify institutional oppression. *Intergroup* oppression occurs when people within devalued groups act out the dominant group's oppression on each other. Examples of intergroup oppression are people of color preferring lighter skin or girls gossiping about each other. Oppression becomes *internalized* when people in devalued groups have heard so many negative messages about their group that they believe the stereotypes about them are true. A working-class person who believes he is not as smart as a middle-class person or a girl who believes she is unattractive because she is not as thin as a model are examples of internalized oppression. *Personally mitigated* oppression occurs when a person of a privileged group makes a demeaning comment to a person in a devalued group. Racial or sexual name-calling, character slurs, or stereotypical assumptions based on social identity constitute personally mitigated oppression.

When individuals encounter oppression, they either accommodate or resist it. *Accommodation* involves accepting or going along with oppression without challenge. Sometimes accommodation is necessary to insure personal safety. *Resistance* involves challenging oppression, but resistance does not have to be confrontational. Resisting oppression can be as simple as responding with "Hey, that's not cool" to a racist joke or sexist comment. Brainstorming possible ways to interrupt oppression provides students an opportunity to generate practical and effective ways to act on what they are learning.

An *ally* is someone who does not belong to an identity group but supports that group's empowerment. Explicit instruction on how to be an ally gives students a way to strengthen and support each other's identities and helps them form relationships across difference. It also helps them understand that social change most frequently results from groups of people forming alliances to create movements.

Students begin to apply these terms to their own experience immediately. In particular, they identify how they have internalized oppression. In the process of identity formation, counteracting internalized oppression is an important skill. Darnell Moore (hooks, 2015) calls the process of overcoming internalized oppression "internal abolition," a process that necessarily begins with recognizing it exists. As Moore says, "We need to know we are bound by something before we can be free of it."

Stereotype Threat

The concept of stereotype threat is related to internalized oppression. Stereotype threat occurs when individuals confront situations in which they are at risk of confirming a negative stereotype about their social group. This is especially concerning when the negative stereotype is related to intellectual competence because it creates a self-fulfilling prophecy. Teachers need to find ways to affirm their students' intelligence and teach them how to counteract stereotype threat. Elliot (2015, p. 140) writes, "By claiming your intelligence, you are manifesting what will happen to you." Steele and Cohn-Vargas (2013) assert that a critical multicultural approach in the classroom helps students from both marginalized and dominant groups develop positive identities and genuine appreciation for others:

> Teachers need to find ways to affirm their students' intelligence and teach them how to counteract stereotype threat.

> Students of color learn to combat stereotype threat and find their voices. All students, whether from dominant or other backgrounds, learn to deconstruct stereotypes and critique their own behavior and what they see around them. This empowerment has an equalizing effect on status for all students.
>
> (p. 83)

Teachers can identify existing communities in the classroom and support diverse identities. Steele and Cohn-Vargas (2013) emphasize the importance of teachers monitoring classroom dynamics, as the social/political dynamics in society are often mirrored in the classroom. Teachers can question social hierarchies and interrupt negative dynamics. They can put students from vulnerable social identity groups in leadership roles that honor their intelligence and sanction their perspectives. They can introduce materials and provide role models to counteract stereotypes, sometimes adding their personal experience into the mix. Oman shares that he believed he was stupid as a child because he was dyslexic. Hearing stories from teachers reduces stereotype threat because it normalizes the experience of identity insecurity, while also demonstrating that oppression can be externalized and overcome.

Teachers need to be humble and recognize that their perspectives are influenced by their social locations. Listening to the voices of others is a crucial aspect of this work. In a patriarchal society, men have been conditioned to be unconscious of women's experience. Likewise, in a racist system, whites have been conditioned to be oblivious to the experiences of people of color. We have to be willing to check ourselves. A teacher can be a highly evolved antiracist and still retain vestiges of sexism. Likewise, a teacher can be a highly evolved feminist and still be under the influence of racism. Teachers make mistakes and, when they do, they can model relational repair.

Family History Projects

Family History Projects introduce students to research and presentation skills, which they use throughout the course. Students begin by interviewing family members about their ancestral heritage. In presentations, they outline their family trees and share interesting family stories. Some students prepare ethnic food to share with the class. After the presentations, the class identifies the countries of origins represented by students' families on a world map. They are fascinated to see the diverse places they have come from as a group and how much of the globe their combined ancestry covers.

Appearances can be deceiving, and students find that their class represents a large and multifaceted group of ancestral heritages, many of which were not previously visible. Multiracial heritages are common, and diverse family backgrounds abound. More families than expected have only been in the United States for one or two generations. Pollack (2008, p. 15) finds that "being more specific about origins allows European American students the opportunity to explore their ethnic identities and ancestries" to "situate them as one among many cultural traditions brought to the United States by immigrants."

Family History Projects connect students' lives outside the classroom to their lives in school. Parents and other family members feel included and involved in the class. Some students contact relatives in other states and sometimes other countries. Students often bring in old photos and historical family documents. They share stories of heroic ancestors, strong female role models, rags to riches stories, and accounts of ancestors who survived the Holocaust, fought for civil rights during the 1960s, or integrated schools to end segregation. Many family stories are about war and conflict, particularly World War II.

Family History Projects strengthen and expand students' identities by connecting them to ancestral heritages and racial/ethnic identities. They learn from their families about the people they come from, and they often emerge from the *Family History Projects* with an altered sense of self. They take pride in telling stories of ancestors who have overcome hardships. They also learn an enormous amount about each other in the process and often view each other differently as a result. Their presentations illuminate differences and allow those differences to become sources of pride.

To end the unit, students reflect on what they have learned about themselves, their families, and others in the class through reflective writing pieces. Olivia wrote:

> I always read stories in books about racism, but hearing about people's ancestors being discriminated against really gave me a different view on it. I wasn't alive during the civil rights act but hearing the stories about people's family made everything come alive in my mind.

Kevin wrote:

> I learned more about my family in that two weeks than I had ever known. Surprisingly, my history was interesting. It made me feel closer to my elders. I also think that my elders felt happy that I took the time to talk to them. I now feel interested and more proud of my history. I learned things that I didn't even think were possible, and that people in my family were well known. They were integrators and founders. I never thought that people in my family could be so cool.

Samantha reported that when she learned her grandmothers on both sides of her family were strong, independent women who immigrated to the United States alone, she wanted to be strong and independent herself.

What students learn about each other's families and cultures brings them closer because they know each other better and can be more understanding. Teachers also learn valuable information about their students' backgrounds, which they can refer to throughout the year. Family history projects allow both teachers and students to see beyond superficial appearances and gain insight into the rich diversity in the classroom.Students often want to continue exploring their heritages through academic research, particularly during the *Peoples' Histories Projects* at the end of the race unit. (See iChange collaborative website (2016) for lesson plan.)

Conclusion

The activities in the introductory unit recursively address the personal, social, cognitive, and action domains of learning. These lessons present key concepts that underpin the TI method and establish clear ground rules for a safe learning community. By the end of the unit, student questions have become more authentic, probing, and sophisticated. Their relationships are closer and more supportive. They are prepared for further inquiries into race, gender, and class identities.

References

Adams, M., Bell, L., & Griffin, P. (2007). *Teaching for Diversity and Social Justice* (2nd ed.). New York: Routledge.

Caldwell, M. & Swift, J. (2003). Beyond "mean girl" typecasting: Power, popularity and potential. *Schoolbook: A Journal of Education, 12*(2), 3–8.

Dubois, W. E. B. (1897, Aug). Strivings of the Negro People. *Atlantic Monthly.* Retrieved from www.theatlantic.com/past/unbound/flashbks/black/dubstriv.htm.

Elliot, S. (2005). *Teaching and Learning on the Verge: Democratic education in action.* New York: Teachers College Press.

hooks, b. (2015). Black Masculinity: Threat or threatened. Scholar-in-Residence Program, Eugene Lang College of Liberal Arts, The New School, New York. Retrieved from www.youtube.com/watch?v=FoXNzyK70Bk.

iChange Collaborative Teacher Resources (2016). Retrieved from www.ichange collaborative.com/ichange/Teacher-Resources.html.

Jones, C. (2000). Levels of racism: A theoretic framework and a gardener's tale. *American Journal of Public Health, 90*(8), 1212–1215. Retrieved from www.ncbi. nlm.nih.gov/pmc/articles/PMC1446334/pdf/10936998.pdf.

Kumashiro, K. (2012). *Bad Teacher! How blaming teachers distorts the bigger picture.* New York: Teachers College Press.

McTighe, J. & Wiggins, G. (2013). *Essential Questions: Opening doors to student understanding.* Alexandria, VA: ASCD.

Pelligrino, J. W. & Hilton, M. L. (Eds). (2012). *Education for Life and Work: Developing transferable knowledge and skills in the twenty-first century.* Washington, DC: National Academies Press.

Pollack, M. (2008). *Everyday Anti-Racism: Getting real about race in school.* New York: The New Press. (Kindle version). Retrieved from Amazon.com.

Siegel, D. (2013). *Brainstorm: The power and purpose of the teenage brain.* New York: Jeremy P. Tarcher/Penguin. (Kindle Version). Retrieved from Amazon.com.

Steele, D. & Cohn-Vargas, B. (2013). *Identity Safe Classrooms: Places to belong and learn.* Thousand Oaks, CA: Corwin.

4

Inquiry Into Identity:
Sample Lesson Plans and
Handouts

Setting the Stage for Inquiry Into Identity

Lesson Objectives

Students will:

- understand the relevance of the course to their lives and education;
- practice speaking and sharing their ideas;
- practice attentive and engaged listening to learn about others;
- reflect on inner thoughts and feelings;
- formulate thoughts and feelings in writing;
- grasp key principles of supportive leadership;
- understand the expectations and outcomes of course participation.

Materials Needed

- "Introduction to Inquiry Into Identity" (student handout)
- "Assessment Rubric" (student handout)
- "What Do You Need to Feel Safe?" (student questionnaire)

Suggested Format

- After welcoming the students, ask them to introduce themselves and share something about themselves (e.g., three facts, what they are looking forward to this school year, something they are proud of, etc., or any other "getting to know you" activity).
- Give students a copy of the "Introduction to Identity" handout. Review each section of the handout with students.
- Give students the "Assessment Rubric" handout and review each component of the assessment criteria.
- Give students a copy of the "What Do You Need To Feel Safe?" and allow 10 minutes for them to answer the questions.
- Ask students to share their answers. Ask one student to be a scribe and take notes on what the group wants and needs. (These notes can be used to create a "Class Contract" as a follow-up activity after Lesson 4.2)

Introduction to Inquiry Into Identity

What Is the Purpose of the Class?

In this course, we explore personal and social identities. We examine social identities (race, class, gender) and the effects they have on individuals and society. Other aspects of identity (religious affiliation, learning styles, language, and even social groups at school) may arise from activities and also become topics of discussion.

How Do You Benefit From Transformational Inquiry?

- You share and learn from each other.
- You learn to collaborate with others to solve important problems.
- You learn valuable communication skills.
- You learn to see things from more than one perspective.
- You learn the power of authentic questioning.
- You learn to use conflict in the service of personal growth and development.
- You learn how to learn.
- You learn how to make a difference in the world.
- You enjoy learning.

What Is Expected From You?

- Honesty
- Openness
- Courage
- Caring
- Commitment
- Respect
- Trust

Do your part to create a safe space for sharing and discussion by displaying the following characteristics:

- Commitment to excellence
- Communication with teachers
- Communication with classmates

Please contribute your highest quality of work through demonstrating communication and commitment in our discussions and in your academic work.

Table Assessment Rubric

CATEGORY	4 – Exceptional	3 – Proficient	2 – Progressing	1 – Developing
Contribution, participation, and engagement	Contributes at a high level. Participates fully in discussions. Leads the way in courage to share personal thoughts, experience, and ideas.	Good contribution. Engaged in class. Shares meaningful information that makes the group safer for everyone. Completes all work.	Adequate contribution. Sometimes shares. Occasionally engages in class. Completes most assignments.	Contribution level leaves something to be desired. Does not communicate feeling or intellectual response, and/or does not complete work.
Leadership and/or initiative	Generates ideas. Takes initiative. Contributes sources. Brings up topics for discussion. Shows courage and integrity. Encourages others. Supports other leaders.	Offers ideas. Takes a role in making sure the group progresses. Supports others in leadership roles. Encourages others to participate.	May come up with some ideas and offer a few suggestions, but mostly leaves it to others to take the lead.	Does not offer ideas or take initiative. Appears disengaged. Undermines group process with inappropriate comments. May undermine leaders and/or teachers.
Listening	Listens attentively to others and responds with supportive feedback. Listens to learn rather than to judge. Questions own assumptions.	Listens attentively most of the time and sometimes offers good comments and/or feedback.	Listens at times, but at other times may seem distracted or bored. Does not often respond to others sharing.	Does not listen well. Talks while others are sharing. Makes unsupportive or inappropriate comments.
Support of others	Encourages others without offering advice or trying to "fix" them. Can see from another's perspective. Can support without agreeing.	Does a good job of compromising and synthesizing ideas with others.	Does a fair job of compromising and synthesizing ideas with other group members.	Can be difficult to work with. Cannot make necessary compromises.
Dependability and trustworthiness	Highly reliable and trustworthy. Helps make the group safe. Contributes their fair share to group projects.	Generally reliable and trustworthy. Respects confidentiality. Contributes to group projects.	Fairly reliable. Learning boundaries around confidentiality and respect. May let others do more than their fair share of group projects.	Unreliable. Does not respect others enough to maintain confidentiality. Contributions to group projects are inadequate.
Attitude	Enthusiastic, encouraging, inspiring, and helpful to others.	Generally upbeat and helpful.	Not especially enthusiastic.	Appears bored, disinterested, or dull.

What Do You Need to Feel Safe?

1. What would you like to get out of participating in this class?

2. What do you need from this group to feel safe to express your authentic thoughts, feelings, ideas, and opinions?

3. What are the most important issues we need to discuss in this group?

4. What gets in the way of talking about these issues?

5. What guidelines can we establish to facilitate a safe environment in which group members can feel safe to talk about their authentic thoughts, feelings, ideas, and opinions?

Creating an Identity-Safe Learning Community

Lesson Objectives

Students will

- understand the importance of supportive peer relationships in an identity-safe learning community;
- practice attentive listening skills;
- practice speaking skills.

Materials Needed

- "Creating an Identity-Safe Learning Community" (student handout)

Suggested Format

- Ask the question "What do you need to feel safe revealing your authentic thoughts and feelings in this class?"
- Allow for periods of silence while students think in order to complete an exhaustive list of characteristics/qualities of a safe learning environment.
- When the list is complete, ask students if they can all agree to the qualities they have brainstormed.
- Give students the "Creating a Safe Learning Community" handout. Go over the material on the handout. Answer any questions. Ask them what they think.

Creating an Identity-Safe Learning Community

Listening

- Be fully present. Pay 100 percent attention. Pay attention to the words, the person's body language, and the energy behind the words. Really listen and try to understand what the person is saying. Your attention creates safety and focus for the entire group.

- Maintain absolute silence when someone is speaking. Side conversations or exchanging looks undermines safety.

- Accept other's sharing without judgment. Don't try to debate, correct, or give advice. Just listen, even if you don't agree.

- Accept yourself and what you feel without judgment. Allow time to process feelings.

- Listening is enough. You don't have to fix anyone. No need to offer solutions.

- Listen, listen, listen, and process what you hear before speaking.

- Allow everyone the chance to speak. Listen 10 times more than you speak.

- If you don't understand, ask for clarification. "Did I hear that right?"

- Treat the candidness of others as a gift and honor their confidentiality.

- Accept conflict as a necessary catalyst for change.

- Be comfortable with silence.

Sharing

- Speak from an "I" perspective. Talk about yourself, not others.

- Talk about experiences you have had rather than sharing opinions or philosophies.

- When conflict arises, express feelings rather than thoughts or opinions. This helps *move through* conflict to new understanding.

- Give feedback offering support and respect.

- If you make mistakes, learn from them, and then let them go.

- Be honest. Say what you think and how you feel.

- Lean into the risk. Get real. Be the one to break it open.

Understanding Emotions as Power

Lesson Objectives

Students will

- learn to identify, reflect on, and discuss emotions;
- begin to understand the role of emotions in learning;
- reflect on what they have learned.

Materials Needed

- "Feeling Power" (student handout)

Suggested Format

- Ask students to complete the "Feeling Power" (student handout) (10–15 minutes).
- Ask students to share their answers in a discussion.
- Give students a one minute period of silence to reflect on what they have learned in today's session. Then ask them to share what they have learned.

Feeling Power

The word emotion comes from the same root as the word motion. Emotions are like fuel; they energize and motivate us. They begin with sensations in our bodies, and if processed, result in insight and learning. If ignored or denied, they keep us stuck in old behavior patterns and can make us feel down and demotivated. Some common ways of processing emotions are talking, laughing, crying, writing, drawing, dancing, and meditation.

- What do each of the emotions look like in your life? What are some ways they can be processed safely? What happens if they are not processed, but pushed away?

    Embarrassment

    Nervousness

    Fear

    Anger

    Sadness

    Grief

- Can you think of other emotions to add to the list?

- Can you think of other ways emotions can be expressed and processed?

- What emotions are easiest for you to express and process? Give an example of a time you felt one of these emotions.

- What emotions are most difficult for you to feel? Give an example of a time you felt one of these emotions.

- How would you describe your relationship with your emotions?

What Is Your Social Identity?

Lesson Objectives

Students will

- explore and reflect on their social identities;
- understand identities as complex matrices;
- understand that some identities are privileged over others;
- understand how identities intersect, are complex, and flexible;
- understand that identities are influenced by society;
- propose theories about why marginalized identities carry more weight.

Materials Needed

- "Social Identity Matrix" (student handout)

Suggested Format

- Introduce the "Social Identity Matrix". Students may need certain categories of identity defined, such as social class, ethnicity, and ability/disability.
- Allow time (15–20 minutes) for students to complete the form. If they have questions about how to fill in the boxes, tell them to just use their best judgment. Avoid answering their questions as the activity is designed to demonstrate that identity is not a simple concept and not always easy to define.
- After they have completed the form, divide them into groups of three or four. Give them 10 minutes to share their matrices.
- After they've had time to discuss their forms in small groups, have them return to the larger class and ask them to share what they discussed in their groups.
- Ask students to identify patterns they observed about the effects of social identities on the people in the class.

Table Social Identity Matrix

Identity How do you identify yourself?	How important is this identity to you? (1–10, 10 is high)	How obvious is this identity to someone who only sees you or does not know you well? (1–10, 10 is high)	How highly regarded is this identity by society as a whole? (1–10, 10 is high)	Ways in which this identity is positively viewed by society?	Ways in which this identity is negatively viewed by society?
Race:					
Ethnicity:					
Social class:					
Gender:					
Sexual identity:					
Ability/Disability:					
Spirituality/ Religion:					
Proposed occupation:					
Membership in social organization/clubs/ sports/extracurricular activities:					
Other:					

5

Inquiry Into Race

A group of African American boys sits in a circle surrounded by their white classmates. Akhil, a high-achieving student and star soccer player, describes being followed through the mall by a security guard. The other boys in the circle nod in recognition. They echo similar stories of clerks watching them in department stores and white women clutching their purses when they pass them on the street. They begin to share the routine dismissals of their integrity and intelligence woven through the fabric of their daily lives. They know they can expect to encounter racism. They have been schooled at home in how to handle it. Trish, however, sitting quietly on the outside of the circle with her white classmates, listening intently, is stunned. She had no idea. She thought racism went out in the sixties with the Civil Rights Movement. Later, the African American boys move to the outside circle, and the white girls move into the center. Now it's Trish's turn to talk about her experience. She's about to find out she's not the only one who didn't know.

SECTION 1: RACE MATTERS

Learning to think objectively about race—to think systematically about racial inequality and to act to overcome racial injustice—requires the courage to explore one's inner landscape, examine the effects of one's cultural conditioning, and act in ways that heal rather than reinforce systemic racism.

In an identity-safe classroom, conversations about race can be productive and enriching for all. When individuals share the ways their experiences are shaped by racial identity, such discussions can yield profoundly unifying results, resulting in stronger individuals and more productive organizations (Berrett, 2012; James & Davidson, 2005; Page, 2007, 2010; Phillips, 2014; Steele & Cohn-Vargas, 2013). Research shows that understanding the dimensions of identity and diversity makes us more creative, diligent, and intelligent (Phillips, 2014).

Race is one of the first things we notice when we meet a person. And while race is only one component of identity, it often drives conversations about identity and diversity. These discussions are necessary, but all too often conversations about race go awry and devolve into confrontation. Conflict avoidance results, and "polite company" goes "color-blind," steering clear of controversy. In avoiding the issue, however, we miss out on real educational opportunities.

What is Race?

The word "race" was originally used to distinguish between people who spoke different languages; hence, Italian, French, Spanish, and English speakers were considered to be of different races, even though by today's standards, they would all be considered white. Many European immigrants arrived in the United States as indentured servants and faced severe discrimination; yet after their terms of enslavement were met, they were free to assimilate into white society. The rise of the transatlantic slave trade in the fifteenth century and the institutionalization of chattel slavery in the United States transformed the notion of race from that of national groups to groups sharing similar physical characteristics, primarily skin color (Omi & Winant, 2015; Painter, 2011). The religious, scientific, and political thought of the era furthered the idea that these corporeal differences signified differences in intelligence, character, sexuality, and temperament, among others. Biologically based notions of race were used to justify slavery, the genocide of indigenous peoples, Chinese and Japanese exclusion, and immigration restrictions (Omi & Winant, 2015). After the abolition of slavery, these notions continued to be institutionalized through Jim Crow laws, debt peonage, unequal treatment in the criminal justice system, unfair housing practices, and lack of access to banking, health-care, voting rights, education, and citizenship. The disparities in economic wealth created by these historical policies are still a persistent reality. Median black wealth, for instance, is five percent of median white wealth, with wealth disparities between whites and Latino and Native Americans being similarly deep (Omi & Winant, 2015).

While racial identity may be a function of the socio-imaginative realm of culture rather than biology, the notion of race has profound psychological and material effects on individual and collective identities. As Leonardo (2013) writes, "Certainly race is a social construction, but its consequences are as real as gravity. Western society may have dreamed up race, but now lives with its nightmares" (p. 14). The legacy of inequality continues to plague society, perhaps nowhere as dramatically as in our schools. Learning the impact of people's histories with an eye toward social justice helps students understand themselves, each other, and the world they live in. They learn to see themselves in the context of a larger social matrix, which helps depersonalize the negative stereotypes they may have internalized. This larger sense of identity empowers them with greater objectivity to think more clearly about the positions they hold in society. The communication skills they learn through conversations with each other prepare them for a changing world in which they will need to understand differences as well as similarities between people.

Race Consciousness vs. Color Blindness

Many of our white students come to us with a "color-blind" view. Like Trish, they believe race discrimination to be a thing of the past and think the United States has substantially achieved a "post-racial" society. Trish's parents rarely talked to her about race, thinking that bringing the topic to her attention would make her racist. Advocates of color blindness, in an effort to be antiracist, feel that the best course of action is to ignore race and treat everyone the same.

In a color-blind society, racial disparities would not exist. Unfortunately, that is simply not the case, and until these disparities can be acknowledged and interrogated, they cannot be changed. Educators who claim to be blind to color are blind to glaring social realities. They are blind to the history, politics, and economics of the United States. Even worse, they are blind to the students standing in front of them who live and breathe the politics of race every day. Racial identity is a lived experience for students of color, and having teachers acknowledge that race exists and that racism is a problem

> Racial identity is a lived experience for students of color, and having teachers acknowledge that race exists and that racism is a problem validates their experience and strengthens their identities.

validates their experience and strengthens their identities. Until racism can be seen, it cannot be addressed. Until it is addressed, it cannot be undone.

Race consciousness, on the other hand, recognizes the significance of race and acknowledges the prevalence of racism in personal, social, and institutional structures. It recognizes inequalities in education, the criminal justice system, housing, and healthcare. Race consciousness highlights differences and disparities and creates an environment in which differences can be met with respect, and disparities can be investigated. It recognizes the intersectionality between identity-based oppressions and emphasizes the importance of solidarity among identity groups, while fostering relationships across difference. Characteristics common to racialized groups emerge as sources of pride, especially when they are cast in the light of political resistance or survival against difficult odds. Race-conscious educators develop the "ability to go through race, rather than around it" (Leonardo, 2013, p. 164).

By bringing the power dynamics inherent in race relations to the forefront of the curriculum, students learn that "structural inequalities help determine personal biographies" (Pollock, 2008, p. 156). Omi and Winant (2015) see racial formation as an ongoing process of individual and collective identity born of conflict and contradiction: between identity and difference; self-reflective action and the structures of society; coercion and consent; and indeed, between the despotic demiurge of the state and the struggle for democracy. And while racial identity is fraught with contradictions, students are fully capable of grappling with the complexity of their own and others' socially constructed, racialized identities. Through personal reflection, sharing stories, exploring academic materials, and participating in action, students learn to position their own identities in the context of a larger sociopolitical milieu.

Racial Identity Development

In the adolescent quest for identity, racial identity looms large for both students of color and whites. Race is a phenomenon we all live within. Pollock (2008) stresses the need for teachers to be aware of students as unique individuals, while keeping in mind the potential effects racialized experience may have had on them. Pollock asserts that everyday antiracism "requires both addressing people's experiences in the world as racial group members and refusing to distort people's experiences, thoughts, or abilities by seeing them only or falsely through a racial lens" (p. xix). Antiracist education rejects false assumptions of difference, but acknowledges that lived experience is shaped along racial lines—whether we have benefited from differential treatment or been harmed by it. Steele and Cohn-Vargas (2013) advocate for educational practices that "enable students to feel that their social identity is an asset, that they are valuable and welcomed members of the classroom, and that they have a range of peer and teacher supports that will help them succeed" (p. xi). Steele and Cohn-Vargas recommend "talking directly with students to learn what they need or think is a good way to avoid being colorblind" (p. 63).

Students of color frequently have a clearer sense of racial identity than whites. White students often do not identify with their race until they encounter material that questions their assumptions. This material can take the form of stories they hear from classmates or academic resources they read and discuss. Students from multiracial or nontraditional family backgrounds may struggle to understand where they fit into socially assigned racial categories that may not reflect their identities.

Students of color learn about the dynamics of racial politics from personal and collective experience. Because they belong to nondominant identity groups, these power dynamics are more visible to them. They engage in frequent family discussions about race, and their parents have taught them to be aware of their racial identities. In some cases, their parents have warned them to be careful around white people (including teachers) and to expect discrimination. Of course, they have also been taught to be proud of who they are and where they come from, and their racial identities have been reinforced and strengthened by their families. Much of what they know about their histories, they learned at home rather than at school.

In spite of parents' best efforts to counteract the impact of race discrimination on their children, students of color, nonetheless, may have internalized negative feelings concerning their identities due to the everyday racism and microaggressions they encounter. Students of color need to have their identities strengthened through positive mirroring from school as well as home because they encounter negative stereotypes so often. They benefit immensely from the validation they receive when teachers and peers listen to their stories, affirm their experience, and support their identities. Because their cultural experience is suddenly at the center of the curriculum, they are motivated not only to learn, but also to teach, often emerging as academic leaders. They benefit not only from having their personal stories integrated into the curriculum, but also from understanding the socio-historical causes of their experience. These students rarely have the opportunity to study the histories of their own people, and

> Students of color . . . benefit immensely from the validation they receive when teachers and peers listen to their stories, affirm their experience, and support their identities.

their identities are reinforced when they see them as a prominent component of academic learning in school. Students of color develop a sense of pride in their racial identities and cultural heritages, which helps them gain agency over their experience. As Carlos wrote;

> I'm mad that I have been taught to be ashamed of my own race, but I'm proud, proud of the culture I bleed, proud of the Aztec warrior blood coursing through my veins. I have brown pride and no one can take that away.

Mariel, an African student, wrote: "I don't think anyone else can be as proud as I am of their heritage and their identity, because in this class I have found a place for my identity and I've learned to love the person that I am."

Many white students come to us in the unexamined identity stage, in which individuals are naïve about the effects of their own identity. They have not questioned the constructs of their racial identity, but instead have accepted dominant cultural attitudes. These students rarely think of themselves in terms of race since white is the "default" identity in the United States. Through a series of activities, they begin to develop a sense of themselves as members of a racial group. When they realize how oblivious they have been to disparities among races, they may initially feel guilty for unconscious complicity in a racist system. Over the duration of the course, however, they come to identify themselves according to values that transcend "whiteness"— as advocates of justice and equality. Through this process, they learn to see themselves as members of a powerful social group, but also distinguish themselves as unique individuals. They learn to think objectively about their racial identities, what they mean, and how they want to express them. As Richard, a white student, reflected:

> I learned that I am one of the people with the best chance of making an impact because I'm a white guy. I also learned it is not my fault. I am not saying racism isn't a white people problem, I am saying I was born into it and I can't help that. I am only doing the wrong thing if I go along with the system.

Like Richard, many white students emerge from the study with an identity that incorporates antiracist activism.

Some students don't fit into governmentally defined categories like Black, White, Hispanic, American Indian, Asian, Pacific Islander, and Alaskan Native. These labels attempt to lump peoples from different regions and speakers of different languages into a single category. The fastest growing demographic in schools today is multiracial students. These students can feel as if they are expected to choose one racial identity over another, so they may need reassurance that identity is individual and can consist of multiple aspects. These students benefit from the opportunity to explore multiple heritages and family structures.

Outcomes of Race Education

All students need to be prepared to negotiate the changing demographics of our nation and world. By mid-century, people of color are projected to make up the majority of the population in the United States (A New Diverse Majority, 2010; Omi & Winant, 2015). Already more than 50 percent of students in public schools are students of color. Students need to understand racial dynamics and acquire social skills that allow them to respectfully learn from people different from them in order to navigate an increasingly multicultural world.

Bullying is frequently related to race, so exposing the power dynamics in social identities can help students modify their behavior and interrupt racism. Support from teachers and peers for a positive sense of racial identity can mitigate the harmful effects of bullying for those who have been its victims and provide opportunities to examine bias for those who have been complicit. Students who feel supported for their racial identities can protect themselves from the psychological effects of intentional racist bullying and the subtle, sometimes unintentional, effects of everyday microaggressions (Sue, 2010) and stereotype threat (Steele, 2011a & b). They find support for processing internalized racism and gain a sense of pride in their cultures. They come to understand that racism says more about the insecurity of the racist than it does about them.

Learning to talk respectfully about race, as well as other categories of identity, can improve school cultures. Steele and Cohn-Vargas (2013) advocate for a "noncolorblind strategy" in which student identities are "validated in the context of cooperative interdependence" (p. 78). Their research shows that by facilitating cross-group friendships and creating an atmosphere of belonging in the classroom, teachers can help students develop a sense of themselves as valued class members, which reduces identity threat and increases academic success.

> **Learning to talk respectfully about race, as well as other categories of identity, can improve school cultures.**

Research shows that students perform best when they connect their identities and lives outside of school to what they are learning. Picower and Mayorga (2015) remind us that this is particularly true for students of color. "Curriculum that connects to students' culture and identities fosters deeper connection to concepts and learning, and can lead to more academic success" (p. 31).

Bellevue Middle School in Nashville, Tennessee identified a lack of knowledge about cultural differences as a key reason students did not feel socially or emotionally safe at school (Orkin, 2012). After students attended a Transformational Inquiry (TI) workshop, administrators reported fewer suspensions and an overall improvement in school culture. Bellevue students reported that they appreciated the opportunity to spend the day learning about each other's lives, gaining insight and understanding into both their similarities and differences. Many of the students wrote thank you notes to the principal, expressing appreciation for the workshop. Students of all races experience increased motivation for learning when they form supportive relationships across difference.

Beginning With Race

We introduce the study of race before we conduct the units on gender or social class for several reasons. We follow the lead of Omi and Winant (2015), who regard race "as a master category of oppression and resistance in the United States" (p. 114). Omi and Winant argue that not only is racial identity a fundamental aspect of human identity, but also that race "has served as a fundamental organizing principle of injustice in the United States" (p. 263). Thus, race not only provides a template for the subordination of other identity groups, but also a template for resistance. The Black Movement after World War II led the way for other social movements to follow in its wake—the women's movement, the student movement, the peace movement, and the gay liberation movement. Other racialized identity groups—Native Americans, Asian Americans, and Latinos—similarly organized coalitions to resist domination and marginalization.

Besides providing a primary template, race is also a visible aspect of identity in most, though certainly not all, cases. The visibility of race makes it more accessible than other forms of identity such as religion or class, which may not be as apparent. As well, it is historically "new," having emerged in the last 500 years. As such, it has a definitive history arising out of the era of exploration and is associated with colonial imperialism. A study of race offers a rich history of resistance and an abundance of material resources for academic inquiry. In addition, the continuing struggle for racial justice is always in the news, making the connections between historical causes and current social issues apparent.

Setting the Stage to Talk About Race

Race is a sensitive subject, but talking about race is not difficult if clear ground rules for respect are established and maintained. Students of color may feel vulnerable sharing incidences of racism, yet when they hear other students share similar experiences, they gain a sense of collective solidarity. When teachers and students outside their identity group validate their stories by listening attentively and giving empathetic feedback, they form supportive relationships and build allied coalitions in their struggle for justice. When students of color see that their personal stories awaken empathy in their white classmates, they feel freer to embrace their racial identities and empowered to express their differences. They are free to express the anger and pain they feel about injustice, and in the process, they gain insight and agency.

White students, who initially feel guilt by association (even if they have done nothing personally to deserve it), may want to dismiss or deny stories they hear from students of color to avoid uncomfortable feelings. They need to understand that internal tension can facilitate dynamic learning if they learn to manage the conflict produced by challenging new ideas.

SECTION 2: TRANSFORMATIONAL INQUIRY IN ACTION

Through the TI process, students come to understand that while race may be a biological illusion, it has profound material effect—not just on society, but also on individuals—and on their identities both personally and collectively. They learn that what they believed to be true about others—and even about themselves—may have been based on faulty assumptions.

TI begins in the personal realm with self-reflection on racial identity. It continues in the social realm with sharing experiences, feelings, and ideas. When "feeling felt" (Siegel, 2014) occurs in the social domain, it reverberates through every other domain. In the cognitive domain, students engage with academic materials that may support or challenge their personal and social insights. Finally, in the action domain, students put their newfound knowledge into effect. They make antiracist commitments, develop strategies for resistance, and support each other in taking a stand against racism. They begin to speak more freely in class discussions, engaging in courageous "speech acts" and revealing ideas they have hitherto been afraid to voice. They produce art, poetry, music, and films that reflect what they are learning. Parents report that they are sharing their insights at home.

Introducing Race

Students begin by investigating terms that will be used in the unit, such as racism, prejudice, and privilege. They review the concepts of oppression, accommodation, and resistance in the context of race. Adelman's (2003) "Ten Things Everyone Should Know about Race" contains important preliminary concepts for talking about race. Opening the floor for students to share previous experience in discussions about race brings out the controversial nature of the subject and reveals the fear that sometimes surrounds such conversations. Students share that they are afraid of being judged and rejected if they say the wrong thing. White students, afraid of being called racist, may hesitate to speak. Students of color are afraid that if they tell the truth about how they feel, they will be contradicted or dismissed. Getting their fears out in the open helps them see that although these kinds of conversations can be difficult, they are necessary and manageable. Knowing their fears in advance allows them to be more forgiving of each other if misunderstandings arise.

A Film Overview

A documentary film can provide a general introduction to current racial issues and concepts. Shakti Butler's (2012) *Cracking the Codes: The System of Racial Inequality* provides an excellent overview and stimulates discussion. Lee Mun Wah's (1994) *The Color of Fear*, a documentary about a group of men (Latinos, whites, blacks, and Asian Americans) who sit down together to talk about race, demonstrates how difficult conversations about race can be resolved in a safe setting. Both films stress the centrality of race to identity in the United States and emphasize the importance of talking about race. Both films model productive dialogues that rivet students' attention. Both filmmakers provide discussion guides and offer film clips online.

Fish Bowls

Students tell us that "Fish Bowls" are the most important activities in the curriculum. (Lesson 5.1, *Fish Bowls* lesson plan, page 106). Members who share the same social identity (in this case, race) form an inner circle. Members of others races form an outside circle surrounding them. Only the students in the inner circle speak during the exercise, and they speak only to each other. They talk about their experiences as members of the group, often responding to an open-ended question such as "What is it like to be a person of color?" (Or black? white? Asian? Latino?) The students in the surrounding circle listen attentively, but do not comment. At the end of an allotted time, students switch places, and another racial group moves to the inside circle. After all the groups have had their time in the inner circle, there is a debriefing session with everyone to give students an opportunity to share their impressions and ask questions across identity groups.

When we conduct this exercise, we separate students by race and gender identity groups. We begin by inviting white males to form the inner circle. For five minutes, they discuss the question "What is it like to be a white male?" while their peers sit quietly outside of the circle and listen. Typically, the white male group has the most difficulty filling the time, and there can be long silences between speakers. Young white men are often at a loss for words in these conversations, as they have not previously reflected on their white male identities and do not necessarily identify their experience as a product of race or white privilege. In most cases, they haven't had to. White male is the default identity in society and where the most social privilege is consolidated. The pauses and silences that permeate the conversation are in and of themselves instructive. They demonstrate a lack of critical reflection and obliviousness to the experience of others, a phenomenon that often accompanies a dominant social identity.

After their time has elapsed, the white males move into the outside circle, and males of color come into the circle. Young men of color usually have plenty of experiences to relate and have no trouble filling the time. They share stories of being called racial slurs, being suspected of crime, having their intelligence questioned, encountering low expectations from teachers, and microaggressions they encounter on a daily basis, such as the expectations that they are athletic or that they are aggressive or angry. They sometimes share advice their parents have given them about how to behave around white people. White students are sometimes shocked to learn that their friends of color experience racism at all and are even more surprised to learn how frequently they encounter it.

Next, white females move into the inner circle. They tend to discuss what it is like to be female without relating much of their experience to their racial identity. Women's oppression is something they feel, so it is more obvious to them. As Patricia Hill Collins (1990) points out, it is easier for individuals to identify their own oppression than to see how their position in society subordinates others. These young white women talk about encountering sexual harassment, not being passed the ball in pick-up games at lunch, how sexual objectification of women in the media affects them, and their fear of rape. Teachers can gently redirect them to the discussion of race or let the conversation take its own course. Ruby Sales, activist and former SNCC organizer, stresses that there is no hierarchy of oppression and that all oppressions intersect all the time. "You can't understand someone else's oppression until you can understand your own," she says (Sales, 2015), so by allowing these young women to feel and voice their own pain, they may be better able to empathize with their classmates' pain of race discrimination. When young white women do talk about race, they typically express that they have little or no sense of racial identity.

Finally, we invite young women of color into the inner circle. These students usually "break it open" because they feel the discrimination of both sexism and racism in their lives. They have the most to talk about and welcome the opportunity to share their experience. Their conversations are the most emotional, and their stories are the most compelling. They share their frustrations at the obliviousness of both whites and men of color to their experience, as well as feelings that their racial experience is trivialized and dismissed by their white female peers. They discuss the effect of being judged by a white standard of beauty, feeling disrespected by men of color, and being seen as exotic by white men. They describe being uncomfortable when white people feel entitled to touch their hair, try to "talk black," and stereotype them as "ghetto." They resent that if they speak up about the discrimination they encounter, they are stereotyped as "that angry black girl." These young women have more awareness of systemic injustice than any other identity group. By the pain they openly display, they invite the other groups to feel with them.

Many of these students have gone to school together for years, and yet because race is so infrequently discussed, they have no idea how much race impacts their lives and relationships. They are astounded to learn how much they do not know about each other. Students of color may be surprised to learn how infrequently white families discuss race because it is so often a topic of conversation in their homes. They are curious about how "white guilt" affects their classmates' capacity for understanding racism, and express a range of reactions from "It's not your fault" to "If you feel guilt, then do something about it." White students are generally surprised to learn how prevalent race is in the minds of students of color, because they seldom have to think about it. Trish remarked:

> When Ahkil and the other boys described walking into department stores and being watched by security guards, I really began to see how their everyday life differed from mine because of the color of their skin. When they described what that was like, I put myself in their shoes and tried to feel how they might feel when things like that happened.

When a student of color "feels felt," it does not matter what color the person who feels with them is. They feel honored and valued by those who listen and empathize. They gain agency when they know that there are others who stand with them.

The "Fish Bowls" exercise creates a profound learning experience. It demonstrates that racism affects all segments of society and makes the subject personal. Listening to and sharing stories is foundational to the TI method, and nowhere is the process more powerful than in "Fish Bowls". The activity engenders respect and compassion in students for the experiences of people who are different from them, and it empowers them to share pieces of themselves that they may never have talked about in a mixed-race group before. Students feel privileged to hear each other's stories and are often moved by them.

"Fish Bowls" can begin with a five-minute time limit for each group. If students want to continue with progressive rounds, the time limit can be extended. Successive rounds of "Fish Bowls" produce deeper material. The activity can be used to explore any social identity. Students sometimes ask for "Fish Bowls" on religion and learning styles.

Intersectionality

Collin's (2009) "matrix of domination" theory introduces the concept that identity is more complex than a single aspect, and instead consists of multiple intersecting components. Because race, class, and gender identities intertwine and overlap in the lives of individuals, Collins argues, racism, classism, and sexism (as well as other forms of oppression) are inextricably bound. Social justice activism must recognize that to eradicate racism, for example, social class and gender oppressions must also be addressed. As the Fish Bowls have already demonstrated, white females are privileged by race, but are subject to sexism. Men of color face racism, but may be oblivious to sexism. Women of color experience both racism and sexism. Gay students of color face the intersection of race and sexuality. Arab Muslims encounter both racial and religious discrimination. Claude Steele (Conan, 2010) asserts that no group is entirely free from negative stereotypes, but when those stereotypes impact them in situations that have consequences for them (such as the classroom, the workplace, or the justice system), they "feel the pressure" of their identities. Intersecting oppressions add to the pressure.

See Baby Discriminate

Bronson and Merryman's (2009) "Even Babies Discriminate" makes the case for why it is important to talk about race (Lesson 5.2, *See Baby Discriminate*, page 107). This assignment includes parents by inviting them to read the article along with their children. Students then interview their parents about how they taught them about race and why. When students share their parents' responses to the interview questions, the differences in conversations about race in families of color and white families are often profound. Students of color report that they talk about race in their families routinely, even daily. Their parents have schooled them in how to negotiate white culture and how to protect themselves from racism. Awareness of race and race identity is already a strong part of their consciousness, as they navigate a society with implicit bias and institutional racism. White students, on the other hand, often report that race is rarely a topic of discussion in their homes. Some white parents even consciously avoid talking to their children about race, because they believe that bringing attention to racial differences could actually make their children racist. Research discussed in the article, however, counters this idea and demonstrates that by not talking about race, white children learn implicit bias. Children can discern racial differences by six months of age, and if such differences are taboo topics, they assume there is something wrong about racial differences. Talking about race actually mitigates bias by bringing conscious attention to differences and making discussions about race a normal part of life.

After reading and discussing this article, students take the online Harvard Implicit Bias test (Project Implicit, 2011). This test measures reaction time to images of faces and gauges bias that may be conscious or unconscious. The results of the test are that most whites and people of color have implicit bias in favor of whites (Banaji & Greenwald, 2013). It is instructive for students to understand that we live in a culture in which our conditioning has made us somewhat oblivious to potentially harmful biases. By knowing, we can begin to deconstruct such biases.

Discussions with students about early memories related to race are also productive. Students of color may describe incidents in which they faced discrimination or were marginalized. They may share experiences of encountering racial slurs from white playmates. White students may share experiences in which they were corrected by their parents for noticing or pointing out racial differences or times they heard adults, sometimes in their families, make racial remarks. When students share these stories, they gain awareness of how their early experience has impacted their identities and relationships.

White Privilege

Learning how infrequently whites discuss racism provides the perfect segue into a discussion of white privilege. McIntosh's (1988/2004) classic article is accessible and provocative. We read this article not just to elucidate the concept of privilege, but also to model active reading, asking essential questions that arise in our minds as we read the article sentence by sentence with students. After the first few paragraphs, we ask students to join in the questioning process. As they share their questions, they become even more involved. We often don't get through the entire article in one class period, because they have so many questions. Their questions include: Must men and whites give up privileges in order for women and people of color to gain privileges? What can whites do to lessen the negative effects of white privilege on other races? How does white privilege hurt whites? Why does racism exist? How can I overcome racism against me? How did racism start? Is it human nature for one group to want to be dominant over another? We make no attempt to answer their questions, but suggest that they keep these questions in mind and allow them to guide our study.

Students of color immediately grasp the concept of white privilege, while some white students struggle to understand it. Because students of color have not been protected from discrimination by white privilege, they see it more clearly. They need to understand white culture to survive, while whites do not necessarily need to understand marginalized cultures. Students of color often take the lead in these discussions, sharing stories, feelings, and perspectives, explaining to their classmates what it is like to be afraid someone will misjudge you because of your skin color, how frequently they ask themselves if a negative interaction happened because of their race, what it means to see negative images of people who look like you in the media, and to be under suspicion when you have done nothing wrong.

White students, on the other hand, find themselves in the position of not knowing that they have privilege and not understanding what it is or how it affects them or how it affects people of color. "I don't get it," Melanie says, "I have never felt privileged." For some white students, particularly high achievers, this may be the first time they haven't been academic leaders in a class, and they are uncomfortable not knowing all the answers. Not only do they not know the answers, but also it is dawning on them that they do not even know what they do not know. Suddenly their eyes are opened to a world they did not know existed, a world in which their classmates of color have lived their whole lives. They realize that "whiteness" has rendered them ignorant and oblivious. Because they have not been affected by race discrimination, they have had the "privilege" of not having to know. They have been protected from having to wonder if they have been slighted because of their race; their parents have not talked to them about how to protect themselves from racism; and they have never worn a Band-Aid that did not match the color of their skin. Karina wrote: "It's been difficult realizing that you have witnessed racism without realizing it, but once you identify it, you can do something the next time, so that's good."

In "Levels of Racism: A Theoretical Framework and a Gardener's Tale," Jones (2000) uses a gardening metaphor, in which particular flowers are planted in richer soil, to demonstrate the effects of white privilege. Her article stimulates deep thinking about the dynamics of race and privilege. Students list five essential questions that arise in their minds as they read the article and bring their questions to class where they read them out loud. Their questions reveal how deeply students think about their lives and the world they live in.

Students expect teachers to answer their questions and sometimes are surprised when they do not. The purpose of this lesson is not to answer questions, but to generate thinking and inspire the quest for knowledge. Besides, these kinds of questions do not have simple answers. They are questions humanity has grappled with for centuries. By simply allowing students to voice authentic questions, teachers invite them to join in the quest to discover their own answers. Reviewing the list of questions at the end of the race unit will show how many of their questions have been answered and how many answers remain unknown. Asking questions is a mysterious process, and they often find answers they did not anticipate.

Because of Martha's identity as a white woman and Oman's identity as a black man, our personal stories demonstrate intersecting oppressions, and our relationship presents a model of how to talk about race and gender. We use our relationship to teach our students about white privilege. Because of Martha's place outside of racial oppression on the matrix of domination, she can support and advocate for people of color without fear of reprisal. When Oman advocates for race, he risks being judged as "having a black agenda" or "making everything about race." Some white students (and adults) find it easier to hear about white privilege from a white teacher because they may identify more strongly with that person. In some situations, a white person talking about racism and privilege still carries more authority. Students of color, on the other hand, appreciate Martha's willingness to confront racism and are gratified that a white teacher can listen, empathize, validate their experience, and offer academic material to substantiate it. Oman can talk about race from a personal standpoint, and his experience validates the racial identities of students of color in a wholly different way. Students of color need to see teachers who look like them, who share their experiences, and can reflect their identities back to them. Oman also challenges white students to grapple with cognitive dissonance around white privilege because they have a personal relationship with him based on mutual care and respect.

Cognitive dissonance often arises from a failure to feel. Some white students are emotionally open enough to understand white privilege immediately, but others resist the uncomfortable feelings that accompany this new knowledge. They resist feeling confused that they do not know the answers, guilty that they have been oblivious to injustice, and sad that racism is a reality for so many people. They may initially deny that racism and privilege exist. They may attempt to minimize its effects with counterarguments that deflect attention from their feelings and move the discussion into the intellectual realm where they feel more comfortable. Privileged groups often "go cognitive" to avoid uncomfortable feelings. Yet, avoiding these feelings stunts growth and protects ignorance. If teachers are savvy enough to redirect these students' attention to their feelings, they can prevent them from derailing the conversation. One way this can be accomplished is through reflective writing outside of class, so that white resistance does not disproportionately consume class time. In one such piece, Edgar wrote, "I feel kind of bad and embarrassed because of my ignorance. But I know I am learning and I did not make the society I am programmed by."

Using class time to focus on defensive feelings has to be balanced with the time allocated to hearing the perspectives of students of color and their allies. Students in privileged positions are accustomed to having their feelings protected, and teachers need to be aware that allowing them too much floor time can actually reinforce racism and marginalize students of color. With encouragement, these privileged students can process their feelings and arrive at new understandings. The underlying reality is that when faced with the knowledge that racism is real and exerts a profound effect on people they care about, white students feel enormously sad.

Step Forward/Step Back

The "Step Forward/Step Back" exercise has a profound emotional impact on students. (Lesson 5.3 *Step Forward/Step Back*, page 109.) Because it reveals the social status of students in the class, we wait until they have some grounding in identity issues before asking them to participate in it, and even then, we let them know they can choose whether or not they respond to particular questions. The exercise encompasses more than just race, and demonstrates the effects of privilege of all kinds.

In this activity, students stand side by side with their arms outstretched. They take the hand of the person on either side of them and hold onto each other's hands as long as possible. The teacher reads a series of statements reflecting the experience of social identity groups. Students respond to each statement by stepping forward, stepping back, or standing still. After the last statement, they look around and observe their different positions. Some students, particularly white males, are near the front of the area while white females and students of color are further back. This exercise makes the effects of oppression visible, showing how it affects members of the class.

The debriefing period after the exercise brings up feelings in almost everyone. Students who end up in the back sometimes, but by no means always, feel self-conscious. Rather than avoiding the exercise for this reason, we instead welcome those feelings. They provide an excellent opportunity for teachers to contradict the idea that those who end up in the rear (due to adverse social structures) are in some way "less than" those who have advantages. We commend those students for what they have achieved. When Amira, a Sudanese refugee, ended up behind everyone else in her class, she told her story in the debrief session. She had overcome enormous obstacles just to be in school and became an instant hero to her classmates. Carlos, a working-class student from an immigrant family, described how he compares himself to others who wear more expensive clothes and live in bigger houses. He shared how hard his father works and how much he wishes he could live like some of the other kids in the class. His peers listened quietly, and then Quinton, a white student, responded. "I admire your father's courage. He sacrifices a lot so that you can have a better life." Unspoken in the room was the knowledge that Quinton's parents, affluent as they were, had divorced the year before, and his father had moved to another state. Carlos later wrote that hearing Quinton say that made him proud of his family and how hard they work. "In some ways," he wrote, "I am the lucky one."

This activity gives teachers the opportunity to voice the value of all identities. Racial identity, like any marginalized identity, can involve stigmatization, but it also comes with a collective identity and frequently with membership in a tightly bonded community of support and resistance. Because identity (and racial identity in particular) is a contradictory phenomenon, there is an upside and a downside to any form of oppression. To strengthen students' identities, both sides of the contradiction must be examined. In this activity, teachers can pay particular attention to the strengths.

Cultural Stereotypes: Race in the Media

There are several films that address media bias regarding race. *Ethnic Notions* (Riggs, 1986) provides an historical overview of African American stereotypes. *Reel Bad Arabs* (Jhally, 2007) is eye-opening in its treatment of Arab stereotypes. *Dark Girls* (Duke & Berry, 2011) challenges the standard of beauty, historically rooted in sex slavery in the Caucasus region (also see Painter's (2011) chapter "White Slavery as Beauty Ideal" in *History of White People*), and examines the effects of present attitudes about beauty and skin color.

Students read several articles about stereotypes and their effects. An excerpt from Claude Steele's (2011a) *Whistling Vivaldi* explains the harmful consequences of "stereotype threat," and Brent Staples's (2010) article "Walk on By" (from which Steele draws the title of his book) gives voice to the concept from a black male's point of view. Teachers can follow up these lessons with web quests in which students find their own examples of racial stereotypes and share them with the class. Some teachers have students create collages of demeaning stereotypical images and contrast them with images depicting people of color as powerful. Students come to understand the profound effects such images have on them and their identities. "I never even noticed these terrible images before," writes Harriet, a white student. "Racism was all around me and I couldn't see it. Now I see it everywhere."

Racial Microaggressions

Derald Wing Sue (2010) coined the term "microaggression," and it has emerged as an important concept in the evolving vocabulary of race-related topics. Microaggressions are subtle, sometimes even well-meaning forms of racialized interactions that insult and demean people of color. Micro-aggressions can take the form of underhanded compliments such as telling an African American that he is "so articulate," or saying, "You speak English so well" to a Mexican American student, or asking an Asian American student "What are you?" Taken in isolation, these statements may appear harmless, but the effects accumulate over time. Students of color encounter micro-aggressions routinely and describe them as "discouraging" and "exhausting." Our students read a pared down version of Wing Sue's article and then visit the *Microaggression Project* blog (n.d.), which contains examples of common microaggressions. The blog's founders invited submissions from individuals who wanted to share their experience and have had over 15,000 submissions (Vega, 2014). Our students share their own stories of microaggression in response to reading the article and visiting the blog.

Web Quests for Statistics on Race Demographics

In a web quest activity, a set of demographic questions guide students to discover race-based inequalities in the United States. (Lesson 5.4, *Wealth, Income, and Social Class Among Races*, page 112.) Economic disparities become obvious when they share their results with each other. Because different sources give different statistics, depending on how they measured the data and how recent the information is, students also learn the value of using multiple sources to examine data in research.

The Visit

After viewing a presentation adapted from Amanda Lewis (2012), author of *Race in the Schoolyard: Negotiating the Color Line in Classrooms and Commun-ities* (2008) and *Despite the Best Intentions: How Racial Inequality Thrives in Good Schools* (Lewis & Diamond, 2015), students engage in an interactive activity that gives them the task of calculating the cost of being African American. The Visit, an activity adapted from A. Hacker's (2010) *Two Nations*, presents a science fiction scenario in which an "official" notifies a white individual that "a mistake has been made." Apparently, he was meant to be black. The mistake must be rectified, and he must become black at midnight. However, the official will compensate him for the costs he will pay for being black. The official asks him for a monetary amount he thinks is fair. Students form small groups and work together to come up with a proposal for the official. They discuss how much they would like to be compensated and give a rationale for the amount they believe would be reasonable. They weigh the effects of race on earning potential, asset accumulation, educational potential, career potential, physical health, housing opportunities, and likelihood of spending time in prison, as well as the psychological effects of racism. After each group comes up with an amount, they come back to the larger group and share the amount they have calculated and their reasons to substantiate the compensation they ask for. Students come up with widely varying amounts of compensation, but the rationales they offer reflect similar reasoning. Inquiring why some groups came up with higher amounts of compensation usually stimulates a healthy discussion and often reflects the emotional underpinnings of their arguments. After participating in this exercise, they better understand the costs of being African American in the United States. The lesson plan, including the slideshow presentation, can be downloaded from the iChange Collaborative Teacher Resources Page (2016). (www.ichangecollaborative. com/ichange/Teacher_Resources.html)

Race in the Criminal Justice System

Racial justice (or the lack thereof) has a long and disturbing history in the United States. Glaring inequities in the rates at which people of color are stopped by the police, searched, arrested, go to trial, are convicted, and sentenced escalate at each step in the legal process (Bobo & Thompson, 2010). The number of men of color in U.S. prisons is widely disproportionate to that of whites. Many of these convictions are drug related and point toward the inequitable law enforcement practices of the War on Drugs. For instance, African Americans comprise only 12 percent of regular drug users, but constitute 38 percent of those arrested for drug offenses and 59 percent of those imprisoned for drug offenses (NAACP, 2015). One of every thirteen black Americans of voting age is disenfranchised due to drug-related convictions, a rate more than four times greater than the rest of the population (Uggen, Shannon & Manza, 2012). African Americans serve almost as much time in federal prison for drug-related offenses as whites do for violent offenses (NAACP, 2015). Two-thirds of people serving time for drug convictions in the United States are people of color (Sentencingproject.com, 2015), and although black people make up only 16 percent of the U.S. population, black children account for 28 percent of juvenile arrests (Report of The Sentencing Project to the United Nations Human Rights Committee, 2013).

The psychological and economic impact of these government policies on black families and communities is devastating, and students need to understand the historical causes and effects. A brief study of the history of the prison system in the United States reveals that prisons expanded dramatically when slavery ended in an effort to reinstitute social control of African Americans (Alexander, 2010). Michelle Alexander (2010), author of *The New Jim Crow: Mass Incarceration in the Age of Color Blindness*, discusses the Schools to Prison Pipeline in an interview students read (Sokolower, 2011/12). They learn that for many young people their age, this pipeline is a reality. The article also makes them aware that activists are attempting to change this reality.

Racial profiling is a common experience for young men of color, and having a safe place to talk about the feelings such treatment engenders helps them process these painful feelings and become more objective about their responses to it. Like us, they are following the news in Ferguson and beyond and need a place to process what they are seeing. For young men of color, bias is not just an academic exercise, but can mean the difference between life and death. Knowing that they have the support of peers and trusted adults to advise them can help protect them from internalizing the images projected on them.

Histories, Research, and Presentations

An authentic question students routinely ask about racism is "How did this happen?" The answer to this question lies in the realm of history. Students research particular racial/national/tribal histories in small, collaborative groups. We encourage them to study a people who reflect their identity because, in terms of identity strength, they benefit most when they research their own heritage. They investigate periods of Black, Latin American, Native American, Asian American, Irish American, Italian American, Chinese, Taiwanese, and Japanese histories, among others. They include timelines in their presentations to the class. These projects teach students research skills, but also give them a larger picture of history because they learn about a number of different people's histories from each other's presentations and can compare similarities in their timelines. As a result, they see larger historical and political trends involving dominance and oppression over time in a variety of contexts.

Teachers can supplement the histories students investigate with lectures on Native American, African American, Asian American, and Latin American histories; immigration history; the history of the prison system in the United States; or the history of court cases related to race in the United States. The history of race itself is also instructive. Teachers need to assess what students know about how government systems operate (separation and balance of powers, difference between federal and state governments, how laws are made, interpreted and enforced) and supplement instruction where needed. Because they apply these concepts in meaningful contexts, students grasp them quickly.

Current Events

Current events discussions need not be confined to a quiz bowl activity or a particular day of the week. Issues concerning race are in the news always, every day, so connections between the history of race in the United States and current events can be drawn on a regular basis. As we write this, the news is replete with issues concerning race: a white gunman killed nine African Americans in a historic black church in Charleston; a white woman posed as black and became president of a local NAACP chapter, protests against police killings of young black men are happening in several cities, and students of color are protesting racism on college campuses.

How to Be an Antiracist Activist

Finally, students want to know how to counter bias, prejudice, and racism. They brainstorm a list of ways racism can be challenged. We stress that personal safety comes first, as there are many ways to interrupt racism without putting one's self in danger. In a collaborative action project, for instance, a group of students posted signs around campus stating statistics on race to raise awareness. They observed other students (and teachers) discussing the statistics and realized they had started a conversation about race.

Inquiry Into Race: Language Arts/English Connections

Poetry, stories, books, and personal essays are excellent ways to supplement an inquiry into race. A timeline of African American history gives context to the Harlem Renaissance, looking backward in time to elucidate the oppression from which Harlem artists were seeking liberation and forward to show the effects of a new black consciousness. Students can read Nikki Grime's *Bronx Masquerade* (2003) and respond to the poems in the book with poems of their own. Sharing their identity-based poems in class is profoundly powerful. Spoken word poetry or slam poetry is another way to integrate identity studies with language arts and segues beautifully from a study of the Harlem Renaissance. Students can watch the spoken work performances of Gil Scott Heron, Suheir Hammad, Saul Williams, and Mark Gonzalez, among others, and contribute their own selections. Watching video performances in class and generating a list of criteria for a good slam—alliteration, repetition, passion, emotional openness, personal stories, clear diction, gestures, and movement—helps them construct their own poems and perform them for the class.

Kidd's *The Secret Life of Bees* (2003), the story of a white girl coming of age in the Civil Rights Era, challenges racism and sexism in religion by presenting a revered Black Madonna deity. Students can research Black Madonna lore from around the world and give short reports. Adiche's *Purple Hibiscus* (2012) examines the psychological abuses of colonialism through the story of a Nigerian family. Adiche's TED Talks—"The Danger of a Single Story" (2009) and "We Should All Be Feminists" (2013)—are excellent supplements to her novel. In Yang's *American Born Chinese* (2008), Alexie's *The Absolutely True Diary of a Part-Time Indian* (2007), Kingsolver's *The Poisonwood Bible* (1998/2008), Potok's *The Chosen* (1967/1987), and Hansberry's *A Raisin in the Sun* (1959/2004), characters explore themes related to racial identity. Short stories such as Hurston's "Sweat" (1926/2008) and Packer's "Brownies" (2003) give students insight into a variety of voices and experiences. The poetry of Maya Angelou, Natasha Trethaway, and Naomi Shibab Nye provoke thought and generate discussion. Films such as *Rabbit Proof Fence* (Noyce, 2002), *The Visitor* (McCarthy, 2008), *Boycott* (Johnson, 2001), and *Selma* (DuVernay, 2014) provide effective ways to integrate themes of race and justice through the power of storytelling.

Conclusion

Using race as a generative theme opens the door to a multitude of possibilities for learning. Because each individual is unique, and each group of students has its own character, it is impossible to predict exactly where the study will lead. Some groups of students thrive in the personal and social realms and gain important, life-changing insights. Others are more affected by the academic content of the course and learn from reading, analysis, and research. The teacher assesses both individual students and the class as a whole to balance the content of the course, moving recursively through the personal, social, cognitive, and action domains for optimal learning. It is the integration of these domains that transforms learning.

References

Adelman, L. (2003). *Ten Things Everyone Should Know about Race*. California Newsreel/PBS. Retrieved from www.newsreel.org/guides/race/10things.htm.

Adiche, C. N. (2009). The Danger of a Single Story. *TED Talks*. Retrieved from www.youtube.com/watch?v=D9Ihs241zeg.

Adiche, C. N. (2012). *Purple Hibiscus*. Chapel Hill, NC: Algonquin Books.

Adiche, C. N. (2013). We Should All Be Feminists. *TEDx*. Retrieved from www.youtube.com/watch?v=hg3umXU_qWc.

Alexander, M. (2010). *The New Jim Crow: Mass incarceration in the age of color blindness*. New York: The New Press.

Alexie, S. (2007). *The Absolutely True Diary of a Part-Time Indian*. New York: Little, Brown Books for Young Readers.

A new diverse majority: Students of color in the south's public schools. (2010). *Southern education foundation*. Retrieved from www.southerneducation.org/Our-Strategies/Research-and-Publications/New-Majority-Diverse-Majority-Report-Series/2010-A-New-Diverse-Majority-Students-of-Color-in-t.aspx.

Banaji, M. R. & Greenwald, A. G. (2013). *Blindspot: Hidden biases of good people*. New York: Delacorte Press. (Kindle version). Retrieved from Amazon.com.

Berrett, D. (2012, Nov 19). Encounters with diversity, on campuses and in coursework, bolsters critical-thinking skills. *The Chronicle of Higher Education*.

Bobo, L. & Thompson, V. (2010). Racialized Mass Incarceration: Poverty, prejudice, and punishment. In H. Markus & P. Moya (Eds.). *Doing race: 21 essays for the twenty-first century*. New York: Norton.

Bronson, P. & Merryman, A. (2009, Sep 4). *Even Babies Discriminate*. Newsweek. Retrieved from www.newsweek.com/id/214989.

Butler, S. (2012). *Cracking the Codes: The system of racial inequality*. World Trust Documentary Films.

Conan, N. (2010, Apr 12). Whistling Vivaldi and Beating the Stereotypes. *Talk of the Nation*. NPR. Retrieved from www.npr.org/templates/story/story.php?storyId =125859207.

Collins, P. H. (1990). Black Feminist Thought in the Matrix of Domination. *Black Feminist Thought: Knowledge, consciousness and the politics of empowerment*. Boston, MA: Unwin Hyman. 221–238. Retrieved from www.hartford-hwp.com/archives/ 45a/252.html.

Collins, P. H. (2009). *Black Feminist Thought*. New York: Routledge.

Duke, B. & Berry, D. C. (2011). *Dark Girls: Real women, real stories*. RLJ Entertainment.

DuVernay, A. (2014). *Selma*. Paramount.

Grimes, N. (2003). *Bronx Masquerade*. New York: Speak.

Hacker, A. (2010). *Two Nations: Black and white, separate, hostile unequal*. New York: Simon and Schuster Digital Sales.

Hansberry, L. (2004). *A Raisin in the Sun* (4th ed.). New York: Vintage/Penguin. (Original work published in 1959).

Hurston, Z. N. (2008). Sweat. In R. S. Gwynn (Ed.), *Literature: A pocket anthology* (4th ed.). New York: Penguin. (Original work published in 1926).

iChange Collaborative Teacher Resources (2016). www.ichangecollaborative.com/ ichange/Teacher_Resources.html.

James, E. H. & Davidson, M. N. (2005). The engines of positive relationships across difference: Learning and conflict. Working Paper Series, paper no. 05–11. Retrieved from www.academia.edu/641672/The_engines_of_positive_ relationships_across_difference_Conflict_and_learning.

Jhally, S. (2007). *Reel Bad Arabs: How Hollywood vilifies a people*. Media Education Foundation.

Johnson, C. (2001). *Boycott*. HBO Films.

Jones, C. (2000). Levels of racism: A theoretic framework and a gardener's tale. *American Journal of Public Health*, 90(8), 1212–1215. Retrieved from www.ncbi. nlm.nih.gov/pmc/articles/PMC1446334/pdf/10936998.pdf.

Kidd, S. M. (2003). *The Secret Life of Bees*. New York: Penguin Books.

Kingsolver, B. (2008). *The Poisonwood Bible*. New York: Harper Perennial Modern Classics. (Original work published in 1998).

Leonardo, Z. (2013). *Race Frameworks: A multidimensional theory of racism and education*. New York: Teachers College Press. (Kindle version). Retrieved from Amazon. com.

Lewis, A. (2008). *Race in the Schoolyard: Negotiating the color line in classrooms and communities*. New Brunswick, NJ: Rutgers University Press.

Lewis, A. (2012). *Whiteness*. Presentation at Paideia School. Retrieved from www. ichangecollaborative.com/ichange/Teacher_Resources.html.

Lewis, A. & Diamond, J. (2015). *Despite the Best Intentions: How racial inequality thrives in good schools*. Oxford: Oxford University Press.

McCarthy, T. (2008). *The Visitor*. Starz.

McIntosh, P. (2004). White Privilege: Unpacking the invisible Knapsack. In P. Rothenberg's (Ed.), *Race, Class, and Gender in the United States* (pp. 188–192). New York: Worth. (Original work published in 1988).

Microaggression Project. (n.d.). *Microaggressions: Power, privilege and everyday life.* Retrieved from www.microaggressions.com/.

NAACP. (2015). *Criminal justice fact sheet.* Retrieved from www.naacp.org/pages/criminal-justice-fact-sheet.

Noyce, P. (2002). *Rabbit-Proof Fence.* Lionsgate.

Omi, M. & Winant, H. (2015). *Racial Formations in the United States* (3rd ed.). New York: Routledge.

Orkin, S. (2012). *Bellevue Middle iChange Collaborative Evaluation.* Bellevue IB Middle School, Nashville TN.

Packer, Z. Z. (2003). *Brownies. Drinking coffee elsewhere.* New York: Riverhead Books.

Page, S. E. (2007). *The Difference: How the power of diversity creates better groups, firms, schools, and societies.* Princeton, NJ: Princeton University Press.

Page, S. E. (2010). *Diversity and Complexity.* Princeton, NJ: Princeton University Press.

Painter, N. I. (2011). *The History of White People.* New York: W. W. Norton.

Phillips, K. W. (2014, Sep 16). How diversity makes us smarter. *Scientific American.*

Picower, B. & Mayorga, E. (2015). *What's Race Got to Do With It? How current school reform policy maintains racial and economic inequality.* New York: Peter Lang.

Pollock, M. (2008). *Everyday Antiracism: Getting real about race in school.* New York: The New Press.

Potok, C. (1987). *The Chosen.* New York: Fawcett. (Original work published in 1967).

Project Implicit website. (2011). Retrieved from https://implicit.harvard.edu/implicit/takeatest.html.

Report of The Sentencing Project of the United Nations Human Rights Committee: Regarding racial disparities in the United States Criminal Justice System. (2013). *The Sentencing Project.* Retrieved from http://sentencingproject.org/doc/publications/rd_ICCPR%20Race%20and%20Justice%20Shadow%20Report.pdf.

Riggs, M. (1986). *Ethic Notions.* Signifyin' Works/California Newsreel.

Sales, R. (2015, Sep 25). U. S. campaign to end the occupation 14th Annual Conference. Atlanta, GA.

Sentencing Project website: Racial Disparity. (2015). Retrieved from www.sentencing project.org/template/page.cfm?id=122.

Sokolower, J. (2011/2012, winter). Schools and the New Jim Crow: An interview with Michelle Alexander. *Rethinking Schools,* 26(2). Retrieved from www.rethinking schools.org//cmshandler.asp?archive/26_02/26_02_sokolower.shtml.

Staples, B. (2010, Sep 9). Just walk on by. *Kelz Mendoza.* Retrieved from www.scribd.com/doc/37177242/Just-Walk-on-by-Brent-Staples.

Steele, C. (2011a). *Whistling Vivaldi: How stereotypes affect us and what we can do.* New York: W. W. Norton & Company.

Steele, C. (2011b). Stereotype Threat and African-American Student Achievement. In D. Grusky & S. Szelenyi (Eds.), *Inequality Reader: Contemporary and foundational readings in race, class, and gender*. Boulder, CO: Westview Press.

Steele, D. & Cohn-Vargas, B. (2013). *Identity Safe Classrooms: Places to belong and learn*. Thousand Oaks, CA: Corwin.

Sue, D. W. (2010). *Microaggressions in Everyday Life*. Hoboken, NJ: Wiley.

Uggen, C., Shannon, S., & Manza, J. (2012). State-level estimates of felon disenfranchisement in the United States, 2010. *The Sentencing Project*. Retrieved from http://sentencingproject.org/doc/publications/fd_State_Level_Estimates_of_Felon_Disen_2010.pdf.

Vega, T. (2014, 21 Mar). Students see many slights as racial "microagressions." *New York Times*.

Wah, L. M. (1994). *The Color of Fear*. Stirfry Seminars and Consulting.

Yang, G. L. (2008). *American Born Chinese*. New York: Square Fish.

5

Inquiry Into Race:
Sample Lesson Plans and
Handouts

Fish Bowls

Lesson Objectives

Students will

- participate in a discussion, sharing ideas and listening respectfully;
- discuss what they observe;
- reflect in writing on what they have learned.

Materials Needed

- Guiding questions

Suggested Format

- Ask members of a specific identity group to come into the center of the room and form a circle.
- Ask other students to form a "listening circle" surrounding the students in the inner circle.
- Introduce the guidelines for speaking and listening for the exercise:
  - Only the inner circle speaks and they speak only to each other.
  - The inner circle shares personal experiences and feelings, but not opinions or philosophies.
  - They allow everyone time to speak.
  - The outer circle listens attentively. They show the inner circle respect by listening silently.
  - After the inner circle shares for the allotted time (5–7 minutes), they move to the outer circle and the next identity group moves into the inner circle.
- After each group has had their conversation, open discussion to the entire group.
- Ask students to write a one-page response describing their insights.

Guiding Questions

- What is it like to be a white male?
- What is it like to be a male of color?
- What is it like to be a white female?
- What is it like to be a female of color?

See Baby Discriminate

Lesson Objectives

Students will

- read carefully and analyze material;
- respond in writing to guiding questions;
- interview their parents regarding race and child rearing;
- participate in a discussion, sharing ideas and listening respectfully.

Materials Needed

- Bronson & Merryman (2009). Even Babies Discriminate. www.newsweek.com/id/214989
- "See Baby Discriminate: Guiding Questions" (student handout)
- Project Implicit website: https://implicit.harvard.edu/implicit/research/

Suggested Format

- Advise students to read carefully as the title is misleading.
- Ask students to answer the guiding questions as they read.
- Review questions 1–5 on the worksheet, which covers content, in a class discussion.
- Ask students to share how their families talk about race and the results of their parent interviews.
- Ask students to explore why parents of different races address the topic differently.
- Ask students to share early memories of learning about race.
- Ask students to explore the Project Implicit website and take several of the tests.
- Ask students if they would like to share any results that surprised them.

See Baby Discriminate: Guiding Questions

1. Why did some of the families drop out of the study on race?

2. Why don't multicultural videos work to change children's attitudes about race?

3. What do the authors believe is the key to changing children's attitudes about race?

4. What is the Diverse Environment Theory? Why does it not work?

5. What are the effects of parents of color preparing their children for racial bias?

6. How often do your parents talk to you about race? What are the conversations like?

7. What are your parents' attitudes about talking about race? Do they feel it's necessary or that it's counterproductive? Please interview them to find out.

8. What is your first memory related to race?

Step Forward/Step Back

Lesson Objectives

Students will

- understand the effects of group identity on social advancement;
- process their impressions in a discussion;
- write a reflective response describing what they learned.

Materials Needed

- "Step Forward/Step Back" statements
- An area large enough for students to form a line standing next to each other and enough room for them to move at least 15 feet forward and 15 feet backward

Suggested Format

- Students stand next to each other in a line, arm's length apart.
- They hold onto the hands of the people on either side of them for as long as possible during the exercise.
- Students remain silent during the exercise.
- If there is information they do not wish to reveal, they do not have to respond to every question.
- Read each statement on the Step Forward/Step Back handout. Each statement will instruct them to either step forward, step back, or stand still.
- When all the questions have been read, ask students to look around and silently observe where they are standing in relationship to other students.
- Conduct a debriefing session.

  - What was that like for you?
  - What did you learn?
  - How do you feel about where you were standing at the end?
  - Are there other questions we could have asked? If so, what are they?

Step Forward/Step Back

If the statement is true for you, take a step forward or a step backward, depending on the instructions.

1. If your ancestors were forced to come to the USA, not by choice, take one step back.
2. If your primary ethnic identity is American, take one step forward.
3. If you were ever called names because of your race, gender, or sexual orientation, take one step back.
4. If people of color have worked in your household as servants, gardeners, etc., take one step forward.
5. If your parents are professional, doctors, lawyers, etc., take one step forward.
6. If you live in a neighborhood where there is prostitution, drug activity, etc., take one step back.
7. If you ever tried to change your appearance, mannerisms, or behavior to avoid being judged or ridiculed, take one step back.
8. If you studied the culture of your ancestors in elementary school, take one step forward.
9. If you started school speaking a language other than English, take one step back.
10. If there were more than 50 books in your house when you grew up, take one step forward.
11. If as a child, you owned more than 6 books featuring characters who looked like you, take one step forward.
12. If you have ever had to skip a meal or were hungry because there was not enough money to buy food, take one step back.
13. If your parents have taken you to art galleries or plays, take one step forward.
14. If one of your parents has been unemployed or laid off, not by choice, take one step back.
15. If you have attended a private school or summer camp, take one step forward.
16. If your family ever had to move because they could not afford the rent, take one step back.
17. If you were told that you were beautiful, smart, and capable by your parents, take one step forward.
18. If you were ever discouraged from academics because of race, take one step back.
19. If you are encouraged to attend a college by your parents, take one step forward.
20. If you have taken a vacation out of the country, take one step forward.
21. If one of your parents did not complete high school, take one step back.
22. If your family owns your own house, take one step forward.

23. If you have seen members of your race, ethnic group, gender, or sexual orientation portrayed on television in degrading roles, take one step back.
24. If you were ever accused of cheating or lying because of your race, take one step back.
25. If your parents or grandparents ever inherited money or property, take a step forward.
26. If you have had to rely primarily on public transportation, take one step back.
27. If you were ever stopped or questioned by the police because of your race, ethnicity, gender, or sexual orientation, take one step back.
28. If you were ever afraid of violence because of your race, ethnicity, gender, or sexual orientation, take one step back.
29. If you are generally able to avoid places that are dangerous, take one step forward.
30. If you have ever been scared to walk down a street at night, take one step back.
31. If you can turn on the television and see people of your race widely represented, take one step forward.
32. If your race and gender is widely represented in Congress, take one step forward.
33. If you have been the only person representing your race or ethnicity in a classroom, please take one step back.
34. If there has never been a U.S. President of the same gender as you, step back.
35. If most American CEOS are the same race as you are, step forward.
36. If most American CEOs are the same gender as you are, step forward.
37. If people sometimes avoid eye contact with you or cross over to the other side of the street to avoid facing you due to your race or gender, step back.
38. If you can't buy Band-Aids that match (more or less) the color of your skin, step back.
39. If you are expected to do more than an equal share of household chores because of your gender, step back.
40. If you have ever felt that you were being closely watched for shoplifting due to your race, step back.
41. If your religious beliefs differ from the majority of people in your community, step back.
42. If you can arrange to be in the company of people the same race as you most of the time, step forward.
43. If you ever felt uncomfortable about a joke related to your race, ethnicity, gender, or sexual orientation, take one step back.
44. If you were ever a victim of violence related to your race, ethnicity, gender, or sexual orientation, take one step back.
45. If your parents did not grow up in the United States, take one step back.

Wealth, Income, and Social Class Among Races

Lesson Objectives

Students will

- research statistics about race in small groups;
- record their sources and compare information with other groups;
- recognize that statistics can vary depending on the source;
- build collaborative skills working in pairs and/or groups;
- weigh the economic effects of racial disparities;
- discuss ideas and listen respectfully to other viewpoints;
- reflect in writing on what they have learned.

Materials Needed

- "Statistics on Race" (student handout)

Suggested Format

- Divide questions on "Statistics on Race" handout among small groups.
- Ask students to research questions and record their source (including date).
- After completing the questions, they discuss their findings with the class.
- Ask them to write a one-page response to what they learned.

Statistics on Race

In groups of two or three, conduct a web quest to find the answers to these questions. Record the source and the date of the information.

1. What percentages of the population in the United States are White, Black, Hispanic, Asian American, and Native American?

2. What percentages of private school students in the United States are Native American, White, Black, Hispanic, and Asian American?

3. What percentages of public school students in the United States are Native American, White, Black, Hispanic, and Asian American?

4. What percentages of the United States Congress (House of Representatives and Senate) are Black, Hispanic, Asian American, White, and Native American?

5. What percentages of Supreme Court justices have been of White, Black, Hispanic, Native American, and Asian American descent?

6. What percentages of Fortune 500 companies' CEOs are Black, Hispanic, Asian American, White, and Native American?

7. What is the average/mean income for White, Black, Asian American, Hispanic, and Native Americans in the United States?

8. What percentages of welfare recipients in the United States are White, Black, Asian American, Hispanic, and Native American?

9. What percentages of your city population are Hispanic, White, Black, Native American, and Asian American?

10. What percentages of students at your school are Hispanic, White, Black, Native American, and Asian American?

11. What percentages of public school students in your city are Hispanic, White, Black, Native American, and Asian American?

12. What percentages of your state's population are White, Black, Native American, Hispanic, and Asian American?

13. What percentages of men incarcerated in the United States are Hispanic, Asian American, White, Black, and Native American?

14. What percentages of death row inmates are Hispanic, Asian American, White, Black, and Native American?

15. Find one more interesting statistic related to race in our country, state, or city.

6

Inquiry Into Gender

A group of girls sits in a circle in the middle of the classroom. Each one takes a turn reading aloud from the open letter they have written to the boys. The boys, sitting around the outside of the circle, listen quietly as the girls list their grievances. Maggie finishes reading her part and passes the letter to Shandra, who clears her throat before beginning the next section. "Putting us down, harassing us, and using us like objects is one thing, but not admitting that you do it is another." She looks up and sees several other girls nodding in agreement.

She passes the letter to Robin, who reads next;

> *When we finally confront you about it in class, you pretend that you have no idea that it happens and talk about putting a stop to it. Then when class is over, you're at it again. You rate girls to boost your masculinity without thought of how it affects us. We want to say something, but we know we'd never be heard or that you'd say, "Stop being so emotional." But you know what? We aren't the ones being overemotional. You are the ones being underemotional.*

Through collaborating to write an open letter, these girls found a collective voice to ask for the respect they deserved.

SECTION 1: GENDER TROUBLE

Gender, like race, is by definition a social construct. While there may be biological variations, these differentiations fall along a spectrum that does not divide neatly into the binary categories of male and female. The term gender refers to socially prescribed behaviors, roles influenced largely by social conditioning. Failure to conform to normative gender roles (binary identity or heterosexual orientation) can result in social consequences, especially during adolescence. Conforming to gender norms, on the other hand, can also have negative effects. According to Laurie Penny (2014, p. 13), "gender is a straightjacket for the human soul."

Gender performances are enacted routinely in the schoolyard to gain status in the pecking order. Steele and Cohn-Vargas (2013) call for teachers to use real-life experiences to question hierarchical relationships, and nowhere is this call more urgent than in gender politics at school. Students strictly police conventional gender norms, and gender-expansive behavior can result in harsh social punishment—ridicule, exclusion, even violence. Research on bullying reveals a clear gender gap: heterosexual girls are harassed at a higher rate than heterosexual boys at every level, with disparities increasing with age (Rich, 2014); 48 percent of students report exposure to relational aggression, a phenomenon ascribed primarily to adolescent girls (Relational Aggression Overview, 2013); 79 percent of LGBT students report being bullied in schools (Prevention of Bullying in Schools, Colleges and Universities, 2013); and 96 percent of transgender students report physical harassment (Sausa, 2005). Research links gender-based bullying to low self-esteem, poor academic performance, elevated levels of depression, and increased risk of suicide during adolescence (Morrow, 2004; Russell, Sinclair, Poteat & Koenig, 2012; Williams, Connolly, Pepler & Craig, 2005; Yunger, Carver & Perry, 2004). Gender-based victimization at school has long-term effects on psychological development that persist into adulthood (Toomey, Ryan, Diaz, Card & Russell, 2010).

Gender conformity, however, also comes at a cost. Young women, conditioned to cooperate, defer, and, maintain an attitude of "niceness," encounter a culture that seeks to both idealize and exploit their sexuality. They find themselves judged by a new standard—attractiveness to men and boys. They may believe that their "nature" is to nurture and plan their futures based on a desire for romantic love. They opt out of higher math and science courses, already planning to subordinate their careers to other's needs. They may not have learned to express anger directly, and may instead subvert negative feelings into acts of relational aggression against other girls, who are safer targets than the boys who demean them.

Likewise, young men, conditioned from an early age to fulfill society's image of a man as a strong, dominant creature, grow up being told to "act like a man" and "big boys don't cry." If their behavior doesn't conform to the conventional male gender role, should they "act like a girl" or "throw like a girl," they risk harsh ridicule from both peers and adults. They learn to mask their pain in order to protect themselves from further social exclusion. The performance role of "unemotional, tough guy" isolates them from others and interferes with authentic relationships. In effect, it isolates them from their selfhood (hooks, 2001). Hypermasculine gender performances repress emotions, stunt intellectual potential, and limit development.

While conversations about gender can begin with the binary categories of male and female, they do not end there. An inquiry into gender leads to questions about gender identity (concept of self as female, male, both, or neither), gender roles (normative behaviors based on binary identities), gender expression (dress, mannerisms, voice, etc.), and sexual orientation (attraction). Questioning gender leads to explorations of gay, lesbian, and transgender issues.

Gender-expansive performance is risky, even dangerous, for all identities and orientations. Homophobia keeps all gender oppression, especially the oppression of men, in place. When students identify with compassion and justice, however, it doesn't matter what their beliefs about homosexuality or gender identity are. They want to take a stand against unfair treatment, whether it manifests as sexism or homophobia.

Young people need to incorporate characteristics from all along the gender spectrum to develop into healthy adults. Young women need to practice speaking their minds directly; they need opportunities to learn how to exercise power (and be valued and validated for doing so); and they need to understand the importance of supporting other girls and women. Young men need to "transgress" conventional gender roles in order to become aware of their emotions; they need to learn to communicate with empathy and understanding, and to make decisions fueled by care for others (hooks, 2004).

> **Young people need to incorporate characteristics from all along the gender spectrum to develop into healthy adults.**

Students who do not conform to conventional gender norms, those who identify as lesbian, gay, bisexual, or transgender, need a safe place to explore their identities.

Gender Identity Development

In the minds of many students, gender norms are invisible assumptions operating below the level of conscious awareness. These students understand binary gender norms to be "natural" and "normal." They have difficulty formulating questions and articulating criticisms that contradict the stereotypical images they see every day in media and in advertising. This constant onslaught of social conditioning creates inauthentic caricatures of gendered identities, which limit their ability to think critically. Students need a safe place to question gender norms and explore the cognitive contradictions and role confusion they experience. Learning to think objectively—to think systematically about gendered identities and to act in ways that heal rather than reinforce gender inequality—is a transformational process that embodies personal, social, and cognitive processes to activate change.

> Students need a safe place to question gender norms and explore the cognitive contradictions and role confusion they experience.

Same-Sex Discussion Groups

Students may feel safer talking about gender in same-sex groups initially. In these groups, girls may feel safe enough to talk about being sexually harassed and not knowing how to handle it; feeling trapped by a double standard, yet feeling powerless to do anything about it; or feeling controlled by media images of female sexuality. Boys may open up about the emotional insecurity they feel about masculine identities, the effects of homophobia, or their confusion about pornography.

The conflict that resulted in the open letter the girls wrote to the boys in the class began early in the year, but so often what goes on in the social realm operates under the radar of teachers. When a group of girls asked Martha if the class could go ahead and start the gender unit, she encouraged them to be patient. We were in the middle of the race unit and still needed to lay important groundwork. The next time they asked, however, she knew something was going on. They told her the boys in the class were rating them based on their physical appearance, discussing their bodies, telling sexist jokes, ridiculing them when they did well academically, and excluding them from sports games. Most of them didn't have the courage to confront the boys, and those who did got shot down quickly with remarks like "Stop PMSing" and

"Why do you have to be so sensitive?" They didn't want the guys to know they had talked to Martha because they were afraid of social retribution.

We immediately shifted gears to address what was happening. We knew, of course, we would need to begin in the social–emotional realm to help them express their feelings. The girls were hurt and angry, and we predicted that the boys would be defensive. To address the need for emotional safety, we decided to separate them into same-sex groups for the first several sessions.

Same-sex groups allow young women to express emotions among other girls, some of whom have likely shared similar experiences of sexist treatment. In conversations, they gain a sense of support when they realize they are not alone. As they hear their own feelings reflected in each other's stories, they come to understand that many of their uncomfortable feelings do not necessarily arise because of personal problems, but may rather be manifestations of a social system that defines their gender identities. In a process that depersonalized their pain and engenders a collective identity, they begin to see their experiences as part of a larger social pattern. LaFrance and Woodzicka (1998) found a correlation between a strong group identity and higher self-esteem among women. They concluded that a strong collective identity protects women from the negative psychological effects of gender discrimination. A collective identity empowers young women to voice the sense of injustice they feel when boys' sports teams get the good practice gyms or when young men make thoughtless comments about their bodies. Monica, a talented swimmer, shared her perception that her coach pays more attention to the boys than the girls on her team. Other girls echoed her sense of unfairness. Monica began to see that she was not alone, that her story was a recurring pattern in a larger social matrix. She realized there was nothing wrong with her personal ability. Perhaps more importantly, in telling her story, Monica realized that her resentment interfered with her motivation and affected her swim performance. Through sharing her experience and getting feedback from her classmates, she gained the psychological distance necessary to recommit herself to her sport. She made an important discovery. Monica realized that the intrinsic reward of doing her best was separate and ultimately more meaningful than any external reward from her coach could ever be.

Through sharing their experience, gender dynamics become visible to girls, and they form important social alliances. The support they gain from each other empowers them to discuss their experience in mixed-gender groups, and when they become more vocal about their experience with sexism, the entire group benefits. The classroom becomes more cohesive and supportive, and the students begin to experience the power of supportive cross-gender alliances. Anthony and Myles, black and white males respectively, were moved by the stories Monica and other girls told about discrimination in sports. They decided to collaborate on a film about sexism in sports. They researched Title IX, interviewed female athletes, coaches, and the owner of a professional women's basketball team.

Young men feel safer in same-sex groups to talk about the pressure they feel to objectify women to gain status in a male-dominated social hierarchy. David, a talented artist, admitted he made crude remarks about girls' bodies to impress other guys because he felt insecure about his own masculinity. Reflecting on his motivation, he realized that he hid his artistic talent. "Art is not manly," he said. "I stopped bringing my sketchbook to school after a guy called me gay in fourth grade." His classmates encouraged him to bring his drawings to school so they could see them.

As teachers facilitating these conversations, we use the knowledge of our own identities and histories. Martha understands how male privilege affects women and girls both psychologically and materially. Oman, as the father of two daughters, is committed to women's advancement. While these combined experiences give us insight into what our students are facing, we also understand that the effects of our own internalized oppression can inhibit our effectiveness in guiding them.

When this group of girls wanted to challenge the behavior of the boys, we decided it would be better for Oman to facilitate their open letter from a place "outside the oppression." When Oman showed Martha the letter, she was surprised by how freely the girls expressed their anger. While anger is an entirely appropriate response to unfair treatment, girls and women learn that expressing anger results in being negatively stereotyped. Martha realized that if she had facilitated their letter, she would have encouraged them to temper their anger to protect them from backlash. Oman, however, freely encouraged them to express their anger because he had not internalized the "angry feminist" or "bitch" stereotype. Thus, he was the perfect ally to the girls because he encouraged them to "tell it like it is." By having Oman's support as a male ally, the young women learned to express their anger in a healthy way. By seeing Oman setting an example, the young men learned to listen to the girls' grievances and understand their positions. The open letter turned out to be one of the most important experiences for our students that year with both girls and boys gaining valuable insights.

Likewise, Martha has not experienced the unrelenting pressure to suppress her feelings to gain acceptance as a man. The negative effects of socially prescribed dominance on men are more visible to her, and her position "outside the oppression" allows her more objectivity. Consequently, she could ally with the boys and effectively guide them to recognize their underlying feelings and help them become aware of their unexamined assumptions about masculine identity. In a brainstorming session, she asked them to list characteristics of a "real" man. "Tough," Matthew began, and other boys agreed.

"Strong," said Brian.

"Independent," offered Cade, "A real man doesn't need help with anything."

"Muscular," said Luke, flexing his thin arm to get a laugh.

"Unemotional," said Brad. "A real man never shows weakness or cries."

"Yeah, we have to push away our feelings," added Steven.

Through this exercise, the boys began to see that the pressure to appear unemotional interferes with authentic relationships—not only with girls, but also with each other. Steven confessed that he actually liked and admired many of the girls in the class, but was afraid to express that because other guys might make fun of him. He felt safer demeaning and ridiculing the girls he admired. Luke shared that he joined in when girls were ridiculed, hoping to gain acceptance from other boys. Daniel said that even though he did not join in, he was afraid to intervene, so he just watched from a safe distance. When Martha asked the boys to reverse the dynamic and express sincere admiration they felt for the girls (rather than the more typical "put downs"), they realized that the behaviors they most admired were not those that conformed to typical gender stereotypes, but rather those that countered them. Brad expressed admiration for Shandra for "calling him out" for sexist behavior. "How else would I know it was wrong? How else could I change?" They talked about the pressures they face to define their masculinity in terms of sexual orientation, their need to guard against being stereotyped as "gay," no matter what their sexual identity is. In order to protect themselves from homophobic slurs, they sometimes adopted a hypermasculine stance. That night Daniel wrote:

> I wish I could live in a world where I don't have to follow these rules to be accepted. I want to be able to express love for my family, loved ones, and friends without getting weird looks. Any show of affection for a male friend and it's "Fag." "Gay." "Queer." Any show of affection for a female friend and it's "Ooh, you *like* her. Are you guys going to start dating?"

He concluded with "All love is outlawed for my gender."

Sexism is painful for everyone. It is painful to be on the receiving end of an attack, but it is also painful to be implicated in the attack. By having the boys focus first on the ways gender norms affect them and recognize how they police each other, they could understand their behavior as conditioned social patterns. From that vantage point, their culpability became depersonalized, and they could own their behavior. Consequently, they were in a better position to hear what girls had to say. It is important for young men to understand their own behavior as "a systemic effect of elitism" and to re-identify themselves as compassionate beings (Penny, 2014).

Outcomes of Gender Education

When gender identity operates below the level of conscious awareness, the effects are felt on both individual and societal levels. Young people understandably fall prey to negative stereotypes, which they either internalize and/or act out on others. Unquestioned gender norms perpetuate a double standard that manifests in unequal division of labor, the wage gap, domestic violence, sexual harassment, rape, and poverty. In a Transformational Inquiry (TI) classroom, girls immediately connect their own sense of internalized oppression to larger social issues: eating disorders, the drop in self-esteem many adolescent girls experience, an artificial standard of beauty relentlessly reinforced through media advertising, and the causes and effects of relational aggression among girls. Boys recognize the effects of emotional suppression and develop strategies to protect themselves from the pressures to conform. They pursue inquiries into gender discrimination, gender stereotypes, gender-based violence, alternative family structures, gay and lesbian rights, and teen sexuality. Through questioning gender norms in an identity-safe learning community, they learn to be allies for each other as they more consciously construct gendered identities, concepts of self that allow for full expression, whether such expressions conform to gender norms or not.

SECTION 2: TRANSFORMATIONAL INQUIRY IN ACTION

Students have already moved through the TI unit on race, so they quickly transfer information about racial oppression to gender oppression, recognizing similar patterns and identifying intersectionalities. Viewing their identities through the wider lens of a social matrix expands their worldview. They not only come to see the world they live in more clearly, but they see themselves more clearly as well.

Introducing Gender

To ground students in the terminology used in the gender unit, they learn to distinguish sex from gender, gender identity from gender roles, and heterosexuality from heterosexism. They conduct web searches in small groups to define these terms, among others. A list of terms and their definitions can be downloaded from the iChange Collaborative Teacher Resources (2016) page at www.ichangecollaborative.com/ichange/Teacher_Resources.html

Students may need to share their fears about discussing gender issues before feeling safe to open up in conversations. Young men may be afraid of being called sexist if they say the wrong thing. Young women are afraid of social retribution if they reveal mistreatment or express anger about discrimination. Getting their fears out in the open gives students a chance to reassure each other and helps them navigate sensitive conversations.

A Film Overview

Documentaries that provide a general overview of gender issues can help set the stage for gender inquiries. *Straight-Laced: How Gender's Got Us All Tied Up* (Chasnoff, Chen, Yacker, Butler & Cutler, 2009) examines how pressures surrounding gender and sexuality affect teenagers along various points on the gender spectrum. *Miss Representation* (Newsom, 2011) addresses media stereotypes and the underrepresentation of women in positions of power and influence. *Tough Guise 2: Violence, Manhood & American Culture* (Jhally, Katz & Earp, 2013) questions outdated models of manhood and critiques cultural messages directed at boys. These films stress the power of media images in the social construction of gender identity. Although students live in a world saturated with media images, they rarely encounter challenges to gender stereotypes. After seeing any one of these films, however, they become highly attuned to media images. They notice the myriad ways in which media depicts masculinity as dominant and femininity as submissive. Students are often shocked to realize the sheer number of stereotypical images they see around them, especially given that they hardly noticed them before. They also begin to question them critically. "Why does this ad for a boat have a photo of a sexy woman in it, but not a boat?" asks Mira.

Fish Bowls

"Fish Bowls" can be revisited in the gender unit and invariably generate riveting discussions. We begin with the binary categories of male and female, while observing that these categories are largely social constructions. If students question or identify outside the binary, they can choose to share in either or both groups. Gender nonconforming students share what it is like to be assigned to a category they do not identify with. Girls talk about the pressure to be attractive and, at the same time, living with a fear of rape and violence that rarely affects boys. Boys talk about feeling guilty and trapped when they succumb to the pressure to objectify girls (who are often their friends and sometimes in the room). Deana wrote that "Fish Bowls" gave her the opportunity to hear the other side of the story:

> I had known a little before about the pressures boys are under to be tough and unafraid, and to not be perceived as "gay," but listening to the fishbowls and taking part in the discussion led me to a whole new level of understanding.

The Fish Bowls activity gives them the opportunity to reflect on socially prescribed gender roles and identify way in which they limit their expression.

Examining Gender Stereotypes: Ideal vs. Real

The "Ideal vs. Real" exercise is designed for beginning gender studies with younger students. We've used the exercise with sixth and seventh graders in mixed- and same-sex groups. It begins with the question "What is an ideal woman?" Students brainstorm answers and compile a list of their responses. After the list is generated, students can form small groups to categorize the items on the list according to: (1) characteristics that are stereotypical; (2) characteristics society defines as ideal; (3) categories men define as ideal; (4) characteristics women define as ideal; and (5) characteristics students believe are truly ideal. The discussion allows girls to think about how gender roles are constructed and how they wish to embody them. It helps boys understand girls' experiences.

Of course, students want to do the same exercise using the question "What is an ideal man?" Young men, too, need the opportunity to look at masculine stereotypes and decide what aspects of socially assigned gender roles they wish to accept and which they wish to reject. Though stereotypes for boys and men are different than those for women and girls, they still generate harmful effects for a lot of young men. Boys who are artistic, who are not athletic, who dance, or who are academically inclined often feel they are not manly enough. They need opportunities to explore the concept of masculinity and re-define it on their own terms.

Gender Oppression: What's Great and What's Not

The "What's Great/What's Not" exercise, described in Chapter 4, is a student favorite in the gender unit. First, girls brainstorm a list of "What's Great" about being female. As they name the benefits of being a girl, we record their answers. Their list includes having more freedom to express themselves emotionally, close relationships with other girls, slumber parties, a wider range of expression in fashion choices, greater permission to express affection, and sometimes the capacity for pregnancy and childbirth. After they have exhausted the list of "What's Great," we ask them to list "What's Not" so great. Their list of difficulties includes feeling judged on looks alone, not "fitting" media stereotypes, the sense that they can never be thin enough, pretty enough, or happy enough, and the fear of being called a "bitch" or labeled a "slut." After the girls exhaust the category of "What's Not," we circle the list of difficulties they have generated. We label this list "sexist oppression." Then they discuss how the entries on their list reflect the four kinds of oppression: institutionalized, internalized, intergroup, and personally mitigated. (See Lesson 4.5 on iChange collaborative website (2016).)

The next day we do the same exercise with the boys. On the "What's Great" side, boys list physical activity, sports, being able to resolve differences with each other directly, less concern for physical appearance, having a sense of personal safety, and the fun they share with each other when being goofy. On the "What's Not" side, they list the pressure to always appear tough, having to watch themselves lest they appear too smart, and having to be careful not to do anything that could be construed as "gay" or "girlie" lest they incur the ridicule of other boys. This allows teachers the opportunity to contradict the notion that there is something wrong with being gay or being a girl.

Students notice several things. First, the girls' list of "What's Not" is considerably longer than the boys, showing that while sexism harms boys, girls bear the brunt of gender oppression. Chelsea wrote that this was one of the most powerful exercises in the class for her: "That's when it really struck me that sexism isn't something that's normal for everyone and it's not something I should have to put up with."

Girls and Self-Esteem/Relational Aggression

Gilligan and Brown's (1998) research brought national attention to the drop in self-esteem many young women experience during adolescence. Seeking social acceptance, they attempt to fit into social norms rather than expressing authentic feelings. They believe they are supposed to be "nice," so they pretend to be, pushing negative feelings, especially anger, underground. This tendency compromises self-esteem because negative feelings, especially anger, are crucial to self-respect and integrity. Girls caught in this dynamic hide their true feelings and have difficulty forming the close friendships they crave.

Because expressing anger directly can feel so risky, some girls opt for superficial relationships based on fear and power. The "mean girl" phenomenon and the drop in self-esteem many young women experience at the onset of adolescence go hand in hand. (Lesson 6.1, *Beyond Mean Girls*, page 140.) It is safer to take out one's aggression on other girls than fight back against a powerful system that assigns greater power to men and boys (or against particular men and boys). Competition for male attention often underlies acts of relational aggression, because boys can bestow power on girls they find attractive. Most girls (and women) have experienced relational aggression, and boys have witnessed it (and sometimes participated in it).

When girls understand relational aggression as a side effect of internalized and intergroup oppression (in which they subvert their anger and act it out on each other rather than express it directly), they can rethink their behavior. Caldwell and Swift's (2003) "Beyond Mean Girl Typecasting: Power, Popularity and Potential" gives students labels to identify their experience and a vocabulary to discuss the feelings that accompany it. Girls recognize experiences similar to theirs in the scenarios from the article and, after discussing it, are in a better position to counter the dynamic by supporting each other's development and success. Alliances among girls and women are important in overcoming sexism, not to mention in creating positive and productive social movements.

Sexual Agency vs. Sexual Objectification

Sexual agency means making conscious decisions about one's sexuality. Both genders need to examine cultural messages that suggest women should be passive and men should be aggressive. Only then can they resist the coercive influence of gender stereotypes and media hype. Madsen's (2014) "On Being Female and Sexual Agency" introduces young women to the language of sexual agency, so they can exercise greater self-determination. Boys, however, feel pressure to establish masculinity through sexual activity (including pornography), so they also benefit from exploring the concept of sexual agency. Kai had never considered that resisting such pressure could be healthier than succumbing to it. "I never stopped to think about how much pressure I get from other guys to go after sex," he wrote in a response to the article. He realized how cultural messages about male identity and peer pressure informed his ideas of gender and sexuality.

Heldman's (2013) TEDxYouth Talk, "The Sexy Lie," explores sexual agency through the question "Is being a sex object empowering?" Heldman introduces the concepts of "self-objectification" and "body monitoring," which girls identify in themselves after watching the video. Alina wrote, "I had never heard the terminology habitual body monitoring before, but I do that all the time. I thought it was just me being weird." Heldman also discusses how men can be involved in counteracting sexual objectification of women. The tension between sexual expression and sexual objectification created ongoing discussions and interesting debates.

The Importance of Male Allies

Presenting the work of male feminists is important because young women need to see men taking leadership roles in the struggle for women's advancement. Young men need positive role models for using their privilege to advocate for gender equality. Tony Porter's (2010) TED Talk "A Call to Young Men" is inspiring in that regard, and Byron Hurt's (2011) "Why I Am a Male Feminist" provides a rationale for self-interested men to support women's empowerment. Jackson Katz's (2012) TED Talk "Violence against Women: It's a Men's Issue" stresses the importance of men's involvement in the movement to stop gender violence.

What Is Power?

Riane Eisler's (2007) "The Feminine Face of Poverty" gives an overview of the material effects of gender disparities. Before reading the article, students research Eisler's life to learn how her personal story influenced her work. Born in Austria under Nazi rule, Eisler escaped as a child with her parents. Her work has been devoted to the question "How can human beings be so cruel to each other?" She postulates a theory of social evolution in which humanity is moving from a "dominator model" to a more egalitarian "partnership model." Eisler's theory introduces students to an alternative way of looking at history, one that questions the assumption that human history is inherently dominator fixed. (Lesson 6.2, *What is Power?*, page 140.)

Reading *The World's Women 2010: Trends and Statistics Executive Summary* (2010) guides students to examine the economic impact of gender discrimination and introduces them to a summary of issues facing women globally. They follow up by interviewing their mothers (or an older woman) about gender oppression she may have encountered in her life. Boys, in particular, are often surprised to learn that their mothers have faced discrimination in education or employment, been sexually harassed, or limited professionally by motherhood. These interviews bring families into the curriculum and make learning personal and meaningful for students.

Stand Up/Sit Down

The "Stand Up/Sit Down" activity (Lesson 6.3, page 142) makes the effects of gender roles visible and personal. Students stand up or sit down in response to a series of statements related to gender identity. Students originally developed the activity, so the statements reflect their genuine concerns. The first set of questions addresses the experiences of young women, and the second set addresses those of young men. The activity has an emotional impact, so students need time to debrief their feelings and share insights. Teachers can conclude the activity by emphasizing the importance of supportive alliances and reinforcing how ally relationships are formed and sustained.

Politics: Material Disparities

Gender roles set up powerful political dynamics that result in material inequalities. In the *Gender Statistics Web Quest* Lesson 6.4 (page 144), students research income and wealth disparities between genders in small groups. The activity offers students insight into how deeply embedded gender issues are in the economy. When students discuss the results of their web quests, they have strong responses to the information they discover. Written responses help consolidate their insights.

Intersectionalities

Gender is only one aspect of identity, and other factors, such as race, complicate the picture. Black girls, for instance, do not experience the typical drop in self-esteem that white girls do (Greene & Way, 2005) and tend to maintain a more positive body image. Colorism, however, does affect young women of color. Alicia, an African American student, initially explored the concept of beauty in her journal, questioning if she could ever be considered beautiful because of her dark complexion. When she was in sixth grade, a boy told her, "You're pretty for a dark skin girl." Alicia internalized this message and felt that because she had dark skin, she could never be beautiful. She began an inquiry study into the intersecting oppressions of race and gender for women of color, and discovered a standard of beauty influenced by a history of white supremacy. She analyzed film and media representations of black women, discovering her own sources and sending us annotated links. She discovered the documentary *Dark Girls* (Duke & Berry, 2011), and found Lupita Nyong'o's stirring acceptance speech for her "Black Women in Hollywood" award (Butler, 2014). Alicia emerged from her study with greater understanding of the social politics of beauty, but more importantly, with the determination to resist cultural stereotypes and define beauty on her own terms. She came to understand that inner beauty is an aspect of character, while outward beauty is a socially and historically constructed norm. Though now in high school, Alicia continues to send us links to articles she discovers in her continuing inquiry. She recently co-taught a short term course on black feminism.

Men of color also face intersecting race and gender issues, particularly regarding stereotypes related to violence and crime. Julian, an African American eighth grader, was almost six feet tall. He already knew he had to be careful not to scare people. He was angry that people assumed he was dangerous, but he was also scared because he knew the real effects that being stereotyped could have on him. He knew the statistics about black men and prison. His dad had been stopped for "driving while black." Julian needed to process his anger and fear, and he needed support from teachers and peers. He also needed information on how to protect himself physically and psychologically from the effects of other people's projections.

Histories

Gender disparities have deep historical roots. Women's issues such as suffrage, reproductive rights, feminism, advancement in politics, law, medicine, business, science, and religion all have rich histories of oppression and liberation. LGBT histories, colonial sexual histories, and the emerging transgender movement are instructive in that students can see how people respond to overcome gender and sexual oppression. The concept of gender itself has changed radically over time, so a survey of gender as a concept is also instructive. Understanding history can empower students to act against oppression rather than acquiesce to it.

LGBT Issues

The presumption that gender identity, gender roles, and sexual orientations are fixed categories is open to question. According to Diamond (2003), "individuals experience a diverse array of attractions and behaviors during their adolescent years, some of which reflect curiosity and experimentation, some of which reflect social pressure, and some of which reflect an underlying sexual orientation" (p. 491). Many students are clear about their sexual orientations, but others are questioning. Gay, lesbian, bisexual, transgender, gender queer, and questioning teenagers need a safe place to explore their identities, and heteronormative teenagers need to learn how to be their allies. Interrupting homophobic comments and gender violence is everyone's concern.

Materials to help students explore these concepts include the articles "Coming Out in Middle School" (Denizet-Lewis, 2009), "What to Do When Your Friend Comes Out to You" (2010), and "How to Be an LGBT Ally" (Miller, 2015). Every year, we invite a panel of gay and lesbian adults, some from our faculty, to tell their stories and answer questions about their lives. These trusted adults talk about when they realized they were gay, how they came out to their families, the obstacles they faced, and how they overcame them. They talk about how their orientations and identities affect their children and families. Students make tremendous gains in understanding as a result of engaging with this panel of "experts." The students comments indicate that following the panel activity, many of them realize that sexuality and orientation are dimensions of love.

Students are questioning the norms of society, but they also may be questioning their own sexuality. With the advent of gay marriage, we see more students openly questioning what sexuality means to them. Even students who identify as heterosexual sometimes choose to write fictional stories from the point of view of a gay or lesbian teenager. Throughout the course we point out contributions by gay and lesbian people in history. We show the documentary *Brother Outsider* (Kates & Singer, 2008), which tells the compelling story of Bayard Rustin, an unsung hero of the Civil Rights Movement. We include literature selections featuring LGBT characters in prominent roles. Excellent information, educational resources, and support for curricula development can be found on the websites of the Gay and Lesbian Alliance against Defamation (2015), Gay, Lesbian and Straight Education Network (2016), Human Rights Campaign (2016), and Gender Spectrum (2015).

Research and Presentation

By this time, students have explored a variety of issues from which to choose a research topic. Girls routinely want to learn how they can rise above gender discrimination. A group who wanted to pursue this question interviewed successful women about how they overcame sexism and gave a presentation to the class. By now, boys are beginning to realize how constrained they are by gender norms and are beginning to identify with a deeper, more aware, and caring aspect of themselves. Students have defined issues and are ready to choose an area of interest to explore independently and may choose topics related to domestic violence, rape, reproductive rights, equal pay, violence against LGBT teens, effects of early sexuality, effects of war on men, sexual harassment, eating disorders, gender roles in Disney movies, standards of beauty, and the effects of media. Students follow the same template for research and presentations they used in the race unit. They learn about a number of topics and immensely enjoy teaching and learning from each other. The research template is available on the iChange Collaborative Teacher Resources page at www.ichangecollaborative.com/ichange/Teacher_Resources.html.

Current Events

A "News Bowl" competition gives students an opportunity to investigate gender issues in current events. They contribute articles on the high cost of motherhood, biological differences, the struggles of gay and transgender youth, bullying, the glass ceiling, the wage gap, and stories of successful women. Current events stories, however, need not be relegated to a separate or culminating activity. Stories about women's issues and LGBT issues are constantly in the news and can be integrated into the curriculum as they occur.

Action Projects

Action can take place informally or emerge organically. As a result of the open letter from the girls and the ensuing academic study, the boys in the class agreed to support each other in countering disparaging comments about women, girls, and homosexuality. They brainstormed ways to "interrupt" gender oppression in non-confrontational ways. After this class session, Scott reported that when he heard boys on his baseball team use terms like "gay" and "fag," he felt strong enough to say, "That's not cool, guys. Cut it out." Eric strongly recommended that the entire class watch the documentary *Girls Rising* (Robbins, 2013). He told the class he watched the movie because he knew the issues the girls described in their open letter were already happening to his younger sister, and he wanted to learn more about issues girls face in other parts of the world. On another occasion, a group of boys came to us privately to discuss a schoolmate whom they knew was anonymously harassing girls online. As a result, the school was able to intervene.

Brad and Steven, who had been involved in rating girls at the beginning of the year, led a collaborative research project on the effects of "macho" stereotypes on boys and men. Their group's presentation to the class outlined much of what they discovered in our discussion, while their academic sources elucidated the systemic nature of their experience. In the spring, they got another opportunity to put what they had learned into practice.

A sixth grade teacher noticed the girls in her class, like so many groups of girls their age, had divided into factions and were enacting typical "mean girls" scenarios in their social relationships. She asked Martha and Jennifer (another identity inquiry teacher) to talk to her students. The sixth grade girls revealed that several months earlier, boys in their class had begun rating them on a scale of one to ten based on appearance. The girls' unexamined reaction was typical: they responded by competing with each other for higher ratings, which translated into higher status in a painful social hierarchy. When we asked, "Who gave the boys the power to rate you?" our question was met with stunned silence. They had never considered that question. We could then talk to them about the importance of supportive relationships among women in a world in which they continue to face inequality.

When our eighth grade students heard about this conversation, Brad and Steven wanted to get involved and talk to the younger boys. They visited the sixth grade class to present their research on male stereotypes. They told the story of how they too had naively rated girls without realizing how hurtful such behaviors were to girls or to them. We subsequently received letters of thanks from the sixth grade students. "I learned so much about stereotypes going around in our world, and it really opened my eyes and made me think," wrote Cassie. "Your eighth graders were so kind and open-minded. It was a great experience for all of us and made our class a better environment for us to come to every day."

The actions these students took arose spontaneously as a result of what they were learning and their desire to share their knowledge with others. Action, however, can be formally embedded in the curriculum through projects and is an essential part of a study that focuses on injustice or inequity among social groups. Students have posted signs to protest gender stereotypes in the hallways at school, organized a movement to interrupt gay and lesbian slurs in online gaming forums, and made films to educate other students about eating disorders.

Inquiry Into Gender: Language Arts/English Connections

Poetry, stories, books, and personal essays are excellent ways to supplement a study of identity. A survey of slam poets such as Sarah Kay, Stacey Ann Chin, and Mark Gonzalez are enough to get students started on a search for poems that reflect their feelings and experiences. Students submit videos of spoken word poets, and we watch a selection of them in class. Students then write and perform their own slam poems.

Writing autobiographical gender stories offers students an opportunity to explore their experience in more depth. Girls write stories about childhood rejection by boys, being sexually harassed at camp, body image issues, or being excluded by a friend who is seeking higher social status. Boys write stories about being teased for not being manly enough, being called gay on the playground, rejecting their mothers (to avoid being called Mama's boys), or disappointing their dads. These stories are right on the surface of their awareness. Ideas for stories may have already emerged from interpersonal activities done in class. Students submit their story ideas in a paragraph and then work with each other in class discussions to develop them.

Integrating gender studies with literature selections stimulates empathy, adds dimension, and strengthens understanding of gender identities. Gould's (1972) "The Story of X" calls the concept of gender into question. Strong female and LGBT characters are trending in young adult literature. *The Hunger Games* (Collins, 2010) and the *Divergent* (Roth, 2014) series are popular among teen readers. Albertalli's (2015) *Simon vs. the Homo Sapiens Agenda* and Chbosky's (2012) *The Perks of Being a Wallflower* feature LGBT characters. For older readers, Morrison's *Sula* (1973/2004), Baldwin's *Giovanni's Room* (1956/2013),

Hurston's *Their Eyes Were Watching God* (1937/2006), or Walker's *The Color Purple* (1982/2003) pose contradictions and provoke insight into gender issues. In Ng's (2015) *Everything I Never Told You*, race intersects with gender.

Conclusion

For adolescents, constructing a healthy gender identity is a key developmental task. Because the task is fraught with so much confusion, especially in today's world, our students need help formulating questions that help them think critically about gender identity, gender roles, and sexuality. Curriculum that begins with personal reflection and moves to social sharing inspires them to question norms and connect academic sources to their own experience. Taking action on their newfound knowledge completes the learning cycle. They emerge with greater agency to resist negative gender stereotypes and construct healthier gendered identities.

References

Albertalli, B. (2015). *Simon vs. the Homo Sapiens Agenda*. New York: Balzer + Bray.

Baldwin, J. (2013). *Giovanni's Room*. New York: Vintage.

Butler, B. (2014, Mar 1). Lupita Nyong'o's speech on "black beauty" underscores her significance in Hollywood. *Washington Post*.

Caldwell, M. & Swift, J. (2003). Beyond "mean girl" typecasting: Power, popularity and potential. *Schoolbook: A Journal of Education, 12*(2), 3–8.

Chasnoff, D., Chen, S., Yacker, F., Butler, R., & Cutler, M. (2009). *Straightlaced: How gender's got us all tied up*. Ho-Ho-Kus. New Day Films.

Chbosky, S. (2012). *The Perks of Being a Wallflower*. New York: MTV Books.

Collins, P. (2010). *The Hunger Games*. New York: Scholastic Press.

Denizet-Lewis, B. (2009, Sep 23). Coming out in middle school. *New York Times*. Retrieved from www.nytimes.com/2009/09/27/magazine/27out-t.html?_r=2.

Diamond, L. M. (2003). New paradigms for research on heterosexual and sexual-minority development. *Journal for Clinical Child and Adolescent Psychology, 32*(4), 490–498.

Duke, B. & Berry, D. C. (2011). *Dark Girls: Real women, real stories*. RLJ Entertainment.

Eisler, R. (2007, Apr 18). The feminine face of poverty. *AlterNet*. Retrieved from www.alternet.org/story/50727/the_feminine_face_of_poverty.

Gay and Lesbian Alliance against Defamation. (2015). GLAAD.org.

Gay, Lesbian and Straight Education Network. (2016). GLSEN.org.

Gender Spectrum. (2015). genderspectrum.org.

Gilligan, C. & Brown, L. M. (1998). *Meeting at the Crossroads: Women's psychology and girls' development*. New York: Ballentine Books.

Gould, L. (1972). The story of X. Retrieved from www3.delta.edu/cmurbano/bio199/AIDS_Sexuality/BabyX.pdf.

Greene, M. L. & Way, N. (2005). Self-esteem trajectories among ethnic minority adolescents: A growth curve analysis of patterns and predictors of change. *Journal of Research on Adolescence, 15*(2), 151–178.

Heldman, C. (2013). The sexy lie. *TEDxYouth@SanDiego*. Retrieved from http://tedxtalks.ted.com/video/The-Sexy-Lie-Caroline-Heldman-a.

hooks, b. (2001). *All About Love: New visions*. New York: William Morrow.

hooks, b. (2004). *The Will to Change: Men, masculinity and love*. New York: Washington Square Press.

Human Rights Campaign. (2016). HRC.org.

Hurston, Z. N. (2006). *Their Eyes Were Watching God*. New York, NY: Harper Perennial Modern Classics. (Original work published 1937).

Hurt, B. (2011, Mar 16). Why I am a male feminist. *The Root*. Retrieved from www.theroot.com/articles/culture/2011/03/why_i_am_a_black_male_feminist.html.

iChange Collaborative Teacher Resources. (2016). www.ichangecollaborative.com/ichange/Teacher_Resources.html.

Jhally, S., Katz, J., & Earp, J. (2013). *Tough Guise 2: Violence, manhood and American culture*. Northampton, MA: Media Education Foundation.

Kates, N. & Singer, B. (2008). *Brother Outsider: The life of Bayard Rustin*. Bayard Rustin Film Project.

Katz, J. (2012, Nov). Violence against women: It's a men's issue. *TEDx*. Retrieved from www.ted.com/talks/jackson_katz_violence_against_women_it_s_a_men_s_issue?language=en.

LaFrance, M. & Woodzicka, J. A. (1998). No Laughing Matter: Women's verbal and nonverbal reactions to sexist humor. In J. K Swim & C. Stangor (Eds.), *Prejudice: The target's perspective* (pp. 62–78). Maryland Heights, MO: Academic Press.

Madsen, P. (2014, Jun 18). On being female and sexual agency. *Psychology Today*. Retrieved from www.psychologytoday.com/blog/shameless-woman/201406/being-female-and-sexual-agency.

Miller, H. (2015). How to be an LGBT ally. *HRC Blog, Human Rights Campaign*. Retrieved from www.hrc.org/blog/entry/how-to-be-an-lgbt-ally.

Morrison, T. (2004). *Sula*. New York: Vintage. (Original work published 1973).

Morrow, D. F. (2004). Social work practice with gay, lesbian, bisexual, and transgender adolescents. *Families in Society, 8*, 91–99.

Newsome, J. (2011). *Miss Representation*. Miss Representation Project.

Ng, C. (2015). *Everything I Never Told You*. New York: Penguin Books.

Penny, L. (2014). *Unspeakable Things: Sex, lies and revolution*. New York: Bloomsbury.

Porter, T. (2010). A call to young men. *TEDWomen*. Retrieved from www.ted.com/talks/tony_porter_a_call_to_men?language=en.

Prevention of bullying in schools, colleges and universities: Research report and recommendations. (2013). *American Educational Research Association*. Washington, DC.

Relational Aggression Overview. (2013). *The Ophelia Project*. Retrieved from www.opheliaproject.org/facts/RelationalAggressionOverview.pdf.

Rich, S. (2014, Jul 29). There's a gender gap in bullying: Watch it widen as kids grow up. *Washington Post*.

Robbins, R. E. (2013). *Girl Rising*. Documentary Group.

Roth, V. (2014). *Divergent*. New York: Katherine Tegen Books.

Russell, S. T., Sinclair, K. O., Poteat, P. V., & Koenig, B. W. (2012). Adolescent health and harassment based on discriminatory bias. *American Journal of Public Health*, *102*(3), 493–495.

Sausa, L. A. (2005). Translating research into practice: Trans youth recommendations for improving school systems. *Journal of Gay & Lesbian Issues in Education, 3*(1), 15–28.

Steele, D. & Cohn-Vargas, B. (2013). *Identity Safe Classrooms: Places to belong and learn*. Thousand Oaks, CA: Corwin.

The World's Women. 2010: Trends and statistics, executive summary. *United Nations Statistics Division*. Retrieved from http://unstats.un.org/unsd/demographic/products/Worldswomen/Executive summary.htm.

Toomey, R. B., Ryan, C., Diaz, R., Card, N. A., & Russell, S. T. (2010). Gender-non-conforming lesbian, gay, bisexual, and transgender youth: School victimization and young adult psychosocial adjustment. *Developmental Psychology, American Psychological Association, 46*(6), 1580–1589.

Walker, A. (2003). *The Color Purple*. New York, NY: Mariner Books. (Original work published 1982).

What to do when your friend comes out to you. (2010). *Youth Pride, Inc.* Retrieved from www.youthprideri.org/Resources/ComingOutAdviceStoriesArt/WhatToDoWhenYourFriendComesOutToYou/tabid/226/Default.aspx.

Williams, T., Connolly, J., Pepler, D., & Craig, W. (2005, Oct). Peer victimization, social support, and psychosocial adjustment for sexual minority adolescents. *Journal of Youth and Adolescence, 34*(5), 471–482.

Yunger, J. L., Carver, P. R., & Perry, D. G. (2004). Does gender identity influence children's psychological well-being? *Developmental Psychology, 40*, 572–582.

6

Inquiry Into Gender:
Sample Lesson Plans and
Handouts

Beyond Mean Girls

Lesson Objectives

Students will

- explore intergroup social dynamics among girls;
- read and answer content and personal exploration questions;
- discuss ideas in class, listening and speaking respectfully.

Materials Needed

- Caldwell & Swift (2003) *Beyond Mean Girl Typecasting: Power, Popularity and Potential in Girls*
- http://www.paideiaschool.org/data/files/gallery/NewsEventsGallery/Beyond_.pdf
- "Beyond Mean Girl Typecasting Reading Questions" (student handout)

Suggested Format

- Have students read *"Beyond Mean Girl Typecasting"*.
- Have students answer the "Beyond Mean Girl Typecasting Reading Questions".
- Lead students in a discussion using the following questions.

  – What was your response to the article?
  – What did you learn that you didn't already know?
  – What is your experience with the "mean girl" phenomenon? How has it affected you?
  – How does internalized oppression result in girls being competitive and/or mean to each other?
  – What can be done to address "relational aggression"?

"Beyond Mean Girl Typecasting" Reading Questions

1. What do the authors believe is the primary motivation for "mean girl" behavior?

2. List at least three examples of "mean girl" behavior from the article.

3. What are girls trying to gain by being mean?

4. What is the cloud of "nice"?

5. What is the most problematic emotion for girls to express and why?

6. What strategies can girls use to move "beyond the superficial level of identity"?

7. What are some positive ways girls can gain power?

8. What is your experience with the "mean girl" phenomenon? Have you ever been the victim of a mean girl? Have you ever been a mean girl? Have you witnessed mean girls in action?

What is Power?

Lesson Objectives

Students will

- use Internet research skills to research and write a biography;
- read and summarize;
- discuss Eisler's concept of history and evolution of human thinking.

Materials Needed

- Eisler (2007), The Feminine Face of Poverty
- http://alternet.org/story/50727/the_feminine_face_of_poverty
- The "Dominator/Partnership Model" (adapted from Eisler & Loye, 1990 (student handout))

Suggested Format

- Ask students to write a half page biography on Riane Eisler using three Internet sources.
- Have them read Eisler's "The Feminine Face of Poverty" and summarize the main points.
- Ask students to share what they learned about Eisler's life.
- Ask students to share the main points of Eisler's article.
- Ask them to share their responses to her ideas.
- Present the "Dominator/Partnership Model" handout and describe Eisler's theory of evolutionary history.
- Conclude by asking students to share essential questions in response to her theory.

Dominator/Partnership Model

Eisler proposes that a new model of social organization is evolving. The Dominator Model has been the prevalent form of social organization over the last 3,000 years, but Eisler thinks it is no longer a workable model. She believes humanity is evolving, and as a result, the Partnership Model will replace the Dominator Model.

Dominator Model	Partnership Model
Power over	Power with
Fear	Trust
Control	Co-existence
Altruism	Alliance
Force	Empowerment
Violence	Empathy
Human nature is selfish	Human nature is caring
Conquest of nature	Respect for nature
Conformity	Individuality/Diversity
Hierarchical	Egalitarian
Obedience to authority	Questions the status quo
Male superiority	Gender equality
Reality is dangerous	Reality is benign
Myths idealize domination	Myths present partnership
Violence is normalized	Peace is normalized
Punishment	Guidance/Education
European history	Multicultural history

Eisler, R. & Loyce, D. (1990) *The Partnership Way: New tools for living and learning, healing our families, our communities and our world*. San Francisco, CA: HarperSanFrancisco.

Stand Up/Sit Down

Lesson Objectives

Students will

- share experiences related to gender;
- discuss their experience, listening and sharing respectfully;
- write a response to the activity.

Materials Needed

- "Stand Up/Sit Down" Statements

Suggested Format

- Read instructions from the Stand Up/Sit Down Statements.
- Read each question, pausing to give students time to stand and for others to take notice.
- At the end of the exercise, debrief using these questions:

  - What did you notice during the exercise?
  - How did you feel?
  - What did you learn?
  - What do you want to know now?
  - What questions would you add to the exercise?

- Ask students to write a half page response to the exercise.

Stand Up/Sit Down Statements

For Girls: Stand up if you have ever:

1. dieted or tried to lose weight;
2. been teased about your body;
3. been harassed sexually;
4. heard people comment on a girl or woman's body in a negative way;
5. felt you were fat;
6. felt stupid because of your gender;
7. been the odd girl out or had a group of friends turn against you;
8. felt that boys or men are smarter;
9. felt that you needed more friends to feel good about yourself;
10. stopped wearing an item of clothing because someone made a negative comment about it;
11. felt disrespected because of your gender;
12. dressed or acted more sexual to be more popular;
13. been told you can't play sports because you're a girl;
14. changed to fit a female stereotype so people wouldn't think you were weird;
15. been so concerned about social issues that it interfered with your schoolwork.

For Boys: Stand up if you have ever:

1. changed your behavior to avoid appearing gay;
2. been afraid of being seen as too smart;
3. felt pressured to join in conversations about girls' or women's bodies;
4. felt guilty for having male privilege;
5. rated girls on a scale of 1–10 based on physical appearance;
6. wished you were taller, stronger, or more muscular;
7. been teased for looking, talking, or acting like a girl;
8. changed your behavior to avoid being seen as a "Mama's boy";
9. been told to stop crying because boys don't cry;
10. been teased because you are friends with a girl;
11. been pressured to go out with a girl;
12. been afraid to be physically affectionate with a friend because it might be construed as sexual;
13. made fun of someone using a homosexual slur;
14. been afraid to stand up to someone when a girl was being objectified;
15. been afraid to stand up for a boy who was being called gay.

Gender Statistics Web Quest

Lesson Objectives

Students will

- collaborate in small groups;
- research statistics using Internet sources;
- report findings to the class;
- discuss their results, listening and sharing respectfully;
- compare sources and variables in statistics.

Materials Needed

- "Gender Statistics" (student handout)

Suggested Format

- Assign groups to collaborate on research.
- Assign each group a series of questions to guide their research.
- After students complete their results, have each team present their findings.
- After each group has reported, ask the students:

  - What have you learned?
  - What do you think now?
  - What do you want to know now?

Gender Statistics

Team One

1. Percentage of female members of the U.S. congress

   Answer: _____

   Source: _____

2. Percentage of female foreign heads of state

   Answer: _____

   Source: _____

3. Percentage of female plastic surgery customers in the United States

   Answer: _____

   Source: _____

4. One other interesting gender statistic that you located

   Answer: _____

   Source: _____

Team Two

1. Percentage of female CEOs of Fortune 500 Companies in the United States

    Answer: _____

    Source: _____

2. Percentage of women and girls living below the poverty line in the United States

    Answer: _____

    Source: _____

3. Percentage of the world's property owned by women

    Answer: _____

    Source: _____

4. One other interesting gender statistic you located

    Answer: _____

    Source: _____

Team Three

1. Average earnings per hour women vs. men in the United States

    Answer: _____

    Source: _____

2. Average earnings per hour women vs. men worldwide

    Answer: _____

    Source: _____

3. Percentage of unpaid labor in the United States performed by women and girls

    Answer: _____

    Source: _____

4. One other interesting gender statistic you located

    Answer: _____

    Source: _____

Team Four

1. Percentage of women who are victims of domestic abuse during their lives

   Answer: _____

   Source: _____

2. Percentage of U.S. children raised by single mothers

   Answer: _____

   Source: _____

3. Percentage of children in the world denied education who are girls

   Answer: _____

   Source: _____

4. One other interesting gender statistic you located

   Answer: _____

   Source: _____

Team Five

1. Percentage of minimum-wage earners in the United States that are female

    Answer: _____

    Source: _____

2. Percentage of American stay-at-home parents that are women

    Answer: _____

    Source: _____

3. Percentage of the world's illiterate population that are female

    Answer: _____

    Source: _____

4. One other interesting gender statistic you located

    Answer: _____

    Source: _____

Team Six

1. Percentage of people living below the poverty line world-wide that are women and girls

   Answer: _____

   Source: _____

2. Percentage of care given to children and the elderly in the United States performed by women

   Answer: _____

   Source: _____

3. Percentage of U.S. millionaires and billionaires that are women

   Answer: _____

   Source: _____

4. One other interesting gender statistic you located

   Answer: _____

   Source: _____

Team Seven

1. Average yearly salary for women and average yearly salary for men in the United States

    Answer: _____

    Source: _____

2. Percentage of the world's working poor that are women

    Answer: _____

    Source: _____

3. Percentage of directors that have won Academy Awards that are women

    Answer: _____

    Source: _____

4. One other interesting gender statistic you located

    Answer: _____

    Source: _____

7

Inquiry Into Social Class

A line of students spans the campus green. Standing side by side, they hold onto each other's hands. Sam, a white male, is standing next to his friend Luis, a Mexican American immigrant. "Step forward if your parents own your home," Oman calls out. Sam steps forward and tightens his grip on Luis's hand.

"Take a step back if your parents work more than one job." Luis takes a step back, and though Sam tries to hold on to his hand, the distance between them is too great, and his grip on Luis's hand slips.

"Step forward if either of your parents has a college education," Oman calls out. Sam steps forward, and as the gap between him and Luis widens, he becomes aware of a sinking feeling in his stomach.

"Take a step forward if you grew up in a home with more than twenty books." Again, Sam steps forward, while Luis stands still.

"If your parents did not grow up in the United States, take one step back." Sam looks behind him to see Luis move even further back.

"Take a step forward if your parents took you to museums, art galleries, or theme parks when you were growing up." Sam moves forward again, becoming further separated from Luis. He looks back and feels conflict. He suddenly realizes how privileged he is. But there are still some students ahead of him. On one hand, he wants to keep up with the kids in front of him. On the other hand, when he sees Luis falling so far behind, he feels guilty.

SECTION 1: QUESTIONING CLASS

Social class is an elusive topic in the United States. Our national myth is that we live in a classless society in which everyone has equal opportunity and hard work pays off. In truth, social class is reproduced from one generation to the next, primarily through inheritance, and is reinforced through an ideology transmitted through schools, religions, governments, businesses, media, and social networks. The contradictory nature of class unconsciousness demands that we reinforce class while simultaneously denying its existence. Barone (2000) captures this irony and its devastating effects: "This dominant cultural mythology, masquerading as reality, has resulted in a crippled conceptual framework for understanding class and an impoverished public discourse on class and classism" (p. 5).

The most affluent one percent of the population controls over half the wealth in the world (Wealth: Having It All and Wanting More, 2015), and the gap between the rich and the poor continues to widen. Between 1979 and 2005, income in the bottom fifth of households grew by an average of $900 a year, income in the middle fifth grew by an average of $8,700 a year, and income in the top one percent grew by an average of $745,000 a year (Putnam, 2015, p. 35). While the causes of this growing gap are debated—globalization, corporatization, the rise of technology, unchecked lobbying practices, failed economic policies—Americans overwhelmingly agree (90 percent) that opportunity, if not wealth itself, should be equally distributed (Putnam, 2015, p. 31).

Schools do not create the opportunity gap, but rather the gap comes to school with the child. The socioeconomic status of children's families is the clearest indicator of how well they will perform in school. There are exceptions, of course, but studies overwhelmingly show that students from affluent backgrounds perform better in school than students from less privileged homes (Cunha & Heckman, 2009; Heckman, 2008; Lanahan, 2009; McLanahan & Percheski, 2008; Putnam, 2015). Ball (2009) suggests that between nine percent and fifteen percent of academic performance can be explained by what happens in school, and class background explains the rest. Families who provide accelerated learning materials, extracurricular activities, travel, exposure, educational toys, access to electronic devices, software, tutoring for learning difficulties, access to better schools, and other opportunities greatly enhance academic success in their children. Students from families without such resources are ill equipped to compete.

> Schools do not create the opportunity gap, but rather the gap comes to school with the child.

What Is Social Class?

Social class is a system that ranks individuals and groups of people according to wealth, income, status, position, and/or power. Upper classes of society control accumulated wealth, usually inherited and built through successive generations, which transfers into significant control over business and political institutions. The middle class aspires to salaried professional and managerial positions, while the working class competes for wage-paying jobs.

Class, however, is a relative thing. There are no concise definitions for class categories as the variables for determining social class are complex. Material possessions can indicate class identity, but so can language, education, family background, and professional status. Class is also determined by access to social capital through clubs and affiliation with social networks. Class identity is subjective in that it is determined in part by how people feel about where they fit in. Income, wealth, education, occupations, and social status fall along a continuum and can change over time.

Class identity, of course, is only one aspect of an individual's overall identity. Within classes, other factors such as race, gender, occupation, religion, sexuality, and nationality form constellations to make up individual identities. Race and gender identities, in particular, intersect with class, because race and gender identities can limit economic potential for individuals and groups. Because material inheritance accumulates in families over subsequent generations, laws that allowed access to wealth acquisition for some and limited it for others have had long-term effects on the potential to accumulate wealth. Laws that restricted home ownership, limited opportunities for education, excluded membership in highly paid professions, and limited political power have institutionalized a class system that intersects with race and gender oppression. These historical factors have manifested stark differentials in income, wealth, educational attainment, and job security. The median wealth for white families is sixteen times greater than the median in black households and thirteen times greater that of Latino families (Sullivan, Meschede, Dietrich & Shapiro, 2015). White women earn 78 percent of what white men earn, while black women earn 64 percent, and Hispanic women earn 54 percent (By the Numbers: A Look at the Gender Pay Gap, 2014). Women's assets likewise reflect the wealth divide. Single women between the ages of eighteen and sixty four have half the assets of single men, and nearly half of black and Hispanic women have zero or negative net worth (Chang, 2010).

Reproductive issues influence the capacity for women to work and accumulate wealth, because the primary responsibility for child rearing is still borne by mothers. More educated women delay childbirth, which increases their opportunities for economic security. College educated women are also less likely to become single parents. They have lower rates of extramarital births as well as lower rates of divorce (Heckman, 2008). In 2004, the divorce rate was twice as high among couples with only high school educations as among those who had completed college (Putnam, 2015). Because two-parent families often have dual incomes, marriage creates economic stability, which benefits children in terms of academic success. Conversely, in lower income families, the stress of economic hardship undermines stability in relationships (Lanahan, 2009). According to Putnam (2015), "poverty produces family instability, and family instability in turn produces poverty. A similar kind of mutual reinforcement occurs between affluence and stability" (p. 74). Family fragmentation, then, has systemic roots and "is powerfully fostered by economic hardship" (p. 79). In 2011, 41 percent of single mothers and 63 percent of children of single mothers lived in poverty in the United States (Casey & Maldonado, 2012), a significant contributor to the overall poverty rate of children, which hovers at a whopping 21 percent of our nation's children (U.S. Census Bureau, 2014).

Social Class Identity Development

Class experience is a fundamental aspect of identity and affects how individuals see the world. The socialization process begins at birth and permeates all classes of society. Langston (1995) describes class as:

> how you think, feel, act, look, talk, move, walk; class is what stores you shop at, restaurants you eat in; class is the schools you attend, the education you attain, class is the very jobs you will work at throughout your adult life.
>
> (p. 112)

While middle- and owning-class people are affected by classism, lower- and working-class people bear the brunt of class oppression. Working-class people are stereotyped as unintelligent, uneducated, lazy, crude, and uncivilized. If students have internalized these negative messages, they may not realize how smart they are. Internalized classism is the means through which people are coerced into agreeing to their own oppression. It limits their capacity to put their intelligence and power into action.

Middle-class students have also been conditioned by classism. They may have internalized the belief they are smarter, more capable, and more deserving of leadership roles than students from lower social classes. They find themselves "caught in the middle" between the social classes above and below them. They may feel superior to working-class people but inferior to those in the owning class; guilty about their privilege, yet worried that they are not good enough. Middle-class conditioning has taught them to cover negative feelings and "put on a happy face." Such pretense takes a toll in spite of the general belief that middle-class people are living the American dream. Underneath the mask, students like Sam fear falling behind, of having less and being less than others.

Cookson and Persell (1986) describe the "prepping process" of upper class students in elite private schools. A system of peer pressure, hazing, a strict code of discipline, and shared rituals produce "deep structural regulation," resulting in a subordination of individual identity to institutional identity or the "systematic wearing down of individual identities into a single collective identity" (p. 35). Owning-class young people are expected to "pay their dues" and emerge from such rites of passages with a mindset of dominance, a collective identity that reflects a sense of entitlement, a loss of innocence, and cynicism. According to Cookson and Persell, "the cycle of socialization recreates generations of individuals whose potentials are often crippled, rather than freed, by privilege" (p. 164).

Outcomes of Social Class Education

Hierarchical structures in social organizations are internalized and become part of individual consciousness, resulting in mindsets in which classist assumptions become fixed. Yet, these mindsets are not immutable and can be transformed through a process of self-questioning, personal reflection, and gaining knowledge about how structural class oppression operates in society. Individuals participate in social institutions by either buying in to classist assumptions without question or by gaining the agency to challenge them.

Young people frequently lack the critical capacity to question class norms. Class identity is the elephant in the room. Our students *feel* it, rather, in their social groups, comparing themselves to others in terms of clothes, houses, cars, even phones. They are keenly aware of who

> Class identity is the elephant in the room. Our students *feel* it, rather, in their social groups, comparing themselves to others in terms of clothes, houses, cars, even phones.

has more and who has less. Media images bombard them constantly with the message that they should aspire to consume more and possess more. Students frequently compare their status to those with the latest electronic devices and expensive shoes, with parents who pick them up from school in luxury cars, or to whom academic success seems to come effortlessly.

When Carlos told the other students about the financial hardship his family faces and how hard his mother works cleaning houses, the feedback he received strengthened his confidence and his appreciation for his family. He heard other students talk about their families and realized that even though his family did not have much money, they were available to him in ways some other students' parents, often busy professionals, were not. In a poem, Carlos wrote:

> This is for you, Mama, for every drop of sweat that's poured from your brow, working to give me a better life, working hours upon hours for minimum wage. I remember driving by those huge houses and asking, Mama, why can't we live in those? I remember moving from one broken down apartment to another. But I promise you, Mama, when I hit gold, I'm gonna buy you the house you deserve.

> **As students share their stories and learn more about social class dynamics, they develop an attitude of resistance to classist patterns of thinking and begin to question economic structures that underlie class disparities.**

Privileged students like Sam reflect on the power they hold due to the circumstances of their birth. They begin to see the bigger picture of how social hierarchies operate in institutions like government, economics, politics, religion, and schooling. Sam, who initially felt guilty for being affluent, shared some words of reassurance his mother had offered: "You can't help how much money your family has, but you can learn to use your money and power to change things." Sam was in the process of redefining his identity and grappling with how to use the power he had.

As students share their stories and learn more about social class dynamics, they develop an attitude of resistance to classist patterns of thinking and begin to question economic structures that underlie class disparities. Demeaning stereotypes in media and in their lives become visible to them. Along the way, many of them commit to each other as advocates, allies, and activists.

SECTION 2: TRANSFORMATIONAL INQUIRY IN ACTION

Class rankings exert a strong influence on the material and psychological lives of our students, affecting not only their life opportunities, but also their self-esteem. Conversations about social class help them identify where they fit into society and address negative messages they may have internalized. Sharing their stories helps them develop empathy and compassion for others, no matter what their social class. Every student is affected both negatively and positively by social class identities, and our work as teachers is to draw out the strengths of their social class positions and reinforce their sense of themselves as worthwhile.

Because our students have already investigated the effects of race and gender identities, they have a background schema for understanding social disparities in society. They understand the effects of marginalized identities on income and wealth distribution, and they understand the necessity of negotiating a positive identity. The recursive nature of the curriculum allows them to draw parallels and see intersections between different kinds of oppression.

Overview of Issues: Film Documentaries

The acclaimed PBS documentary *People Like Us: Social Class in America* (Alvarez & Kolker, 2001) gives students an overview of class issues and provides context for how class identity affects people at all levels of society. If this film is not available in your library, clips are available online. Students particularly relate to the segment about social class rankings in high schools. After viewing the film, they share their responses in a class discussion.

Defining Our Terms

Our students frequently do not understand class distinctions, so they need an introduction to key terms such as working class, middle class, owning class, underclass, blue collar, and white collar, as well as some basic vocabulary in economics. Because many of these terms do not have hard and fast definitions, collaborating in small groups to find Internet sources to define them helps students consolidate their meanings. When the groups share the definitions they have found with the class, they see that these terms have amorphous meanings with different sources offering different criteria of distinctions. (See list of terms in Lesson 7.0 on iChange website (2016).)

Exploring Class Stereotypes

In an activity designed to elucidate class stereotypes, students work in groups to generate positive and negative characteristics they associate with each social class: upper, middle, and lower. They compare and contrast the list of traits they associate with each class, most of which are stereotypical. They can also reflect on where their ideas come from: family, school, media, or personal experience. (Lesson 7.1 Social Class Catagories, page 171.)

Media Analysis: Busting Stereotypes

Upper-class snobs, trailer trash, ignorant red necks, ghetto dwellers, poor but noble, and working-class stiffs are all labels associated with class status. The article "Mass Media and Images of Social Class" (Newman, 2006) provides a brief introduction to media issues related to social class. "Media Magic— Making Class Invisible" (Mantsio, 1995) argues that images of the poor are largely absent in media, obscuring understanding and preventing social action on their behalf. Readings of one or both of these articles, followed by web searches in which students find images that either support or contradict the ideas presented, attune them to the social class stereotypes that surround them.

The Money Game

Class is determined, in part, by the amount of money people earn, but values determine how people spend money. The Money Game taps into the psychological value of money and stimulates thinking about economics and finance. Students spend imaginary money in increasing amounts throughout the game. Each week they receive a deposit, and they can spend their virtual money on anything they want. Because they are given money in amounts too large for someone their age to spend, they eventually have to think about how to spend money on a larger social scale (or at least most of them do). How they choose to spend, save, invest, or give away money reveals underlying values associated with material and social wealth.

The first week they get $10,000, and they shop online to their heart's content. The second week they get $100,000, and now they are looking to the future. The third week they get $1,000,000, and now they can live a life of luxury. The game continues with weekly awards of $10,000,000, $100,000,000, and $1,000,000,000. They keep a record of how they spend the money, documenting as accurately as possible the cost of the items or experiences they buy and submit a weekly report. In addition to their ledger of income and expenses, they reflect on their feelings about how they spent their money during the week and record any insights they may have had. Teachers can help them recognize how deeper desires are translated into how one spends money. This activity stimulates thought about how money works in the world. Some students use their imaginary money to address solutions to social problems, giving to charity, or creating imaginary foundations. Some share money and collaborate on joint projects. Bianca recruited classmates to collaborate on how to alleviate world hunger. The group figured out how much it would cost and realized they would have to come up with other means of funding. They looked at the federal budget and considered how taxes could be distributed fairly.

Questioning Class: Personal Reflections

The "Questioning Class" exercise (Jackson, 2010) gives students an opportunity to examine their values related to social class identity (Lesson 7.3, page 172). Students share their answers to the questions in class. They typically share that they feel embarrassed or guilty about their social class no matter what their class identity. Kevin, an upper-class student wrote:

> I feel guilty for having more than I should and that I've been given a big head start in life. I've also got a big safety net that I don't really want, I know that if I was stupid or for whatever reason wasn't successful despite the great education I'll have, my parents would give me money and continue to support me, which is a privilege that so many people don't have and I feel guilty for having it.

Heather gives a view from the middle class:

> There are actually some friends I don't like to go shopping with because I feel way too awkward when they leave the mall with four or five shopping bags and I have one or none. On the other hand, these same friends can be very generous. I don't think they see me as a charity case, but sometimes I feel like one.

Heather also shares that she has friends from lower socioeconomic classes: "The media portrays people in a low class as stupid, but a lot of people I know in lower classes are smarter than me and some of them are the smartest people I know."

In a follow-up activity, students reflect on a time they were aware that people around them had considerably more wealth than they did. They reflect for a few minutes and then write a paragraph about the feelings that accompanied their reflections. Next they remember a time they were aware that people around them had considerably less wealth than they did, and then they write about their feelings in that situation. Sharing their experiences and their feelings highlights the emotional complexity of class identity. When asked how they identified their relative class rankings in their scenarios, they name class indicators such as clothing, housing, language, education, regional dialects, vocabulary, hobbies, recreational activities, travel, electronic devices, or cars.

For some groups, "The Affluence Questionnaire" (O'Neill, 1997) may be appropriate. In this inventory, students explore ways in which having wealth and belonging to an upper-level social class can affect identity, self-esteem, and relationships. Seeing upper-class people as only privileged obscures the negative dimensions the class system has on all levels of society.

Fish Bowls

Students participate in "Fish Bowls" based on how they self-identify, choosing to participate in upper-class, middle-class, or lower-class conversation. The majority of students identify as middle class, whether they are actually middle class or not. The "Fish Bowls" reveal that they worry about their peers finding them unacceptable either for what they have or for what they do not have. If they identify as upper class, they may feel guilty for having too much; lower-class students may feel embarrassed for not having enough; and middle-class students feel guilty for having less than affluent and more than working-class students. They recognize their own uneasiness in each other's stories, and the invisible structures of social class operating in their relationships come into view.

Readings in Social Class

The interactive activities create meaningful contexts for understanding reading materials. Paul Fussell's (1992) description of American attitudes about social class in "A Touchy Subject" provides an introduction to many of the ideas presented in this unit. Killerman's (2012) list of "30+ Examples of Middle and Upper Class Privilege" connects the concept of privilege, already introduced in the race and gender units, to class identities. Anderson's (2012) "Seeing Through the Privilege Haze" gives a specific context to illustrate the concept. Articles examining issues affecting particular class categories extend and clarify these concepts. Bobo's (1993) "Pride, Prejudice and the Not-So-Subtle Politics of the Working Class" examines the way dress relates to occupational status. Brownstein's (2013) "Meet the New Middle Class" takes a look at changing economic trends that affect class status, and Fabrikant's (2005) "Old Nantucket Warily Meets New" examines the conflict between old money and new money within the upper class.

Histories of Class in America

Class issues in the United States have deep historical roots. Students cannot begin to understand how to generate solutions to problems unless they understand how these problems have evolved through time. Through learning histories, they acquire the foundation for generating solutions to complex social problems. The histories of capitalism, the banking system, the industrial revolution, the Labor Movement, socialism, and communism can provide rich and rewarding material for study. The history behind the campaign for the 40-hour workweek, the struggle to outlaw child labor, and the movements to create workers' compensation and unemployment laws can introduce students to political movements in ongoing class struggles. Learning the causes and effects of the Great Depression, a study of the New Deal, or the War on Poverty can provide students with understanding of the ways political movements influence governments and economies. Counter movements, as well (Nixon's Southern Strategy, Reagan's Trickle Down economic policies, and the rise of the Moral Majority or the Tea Party), demonstrate the back and forth movement between political groups with differing visions of society. An investigation into the Supreme Court decision on Citizen's United and the subsequent effect on politics in the United States helps students understand the influence wealth exerts on government officials through the election process. A look at the enduring economic effects of slavery and racism on wealth accumulation for African American families is also instructive, particularly as it shows the intersection of race and class. The history of class itself and changing ideas about classism make worthy inquiry topics.

Politics: Researching Material Disparities

Researching statistics related to social class demographics is an eye-opening experience for students. (Lesson 7.4, Social Class Statistics Web Quest, page 174.) Students explore and compare income and wealth statistics in small groups using Internet sources. They discover sources that conflict and find information influenced by political bias. They begin to question how the playing field for wealth and social status can be equalized.

Redistribution of Wealth

The term "redistribution of wealth" strikes fear at the heart of U.S. politics. While redistribution of wealth is generally associated with social programs like food stamps, Medicare, and Medicaid, in reality, the United States government spends far more (almost $100 billion) on federal tax breaks for corporations than on social programs (Detlaven, 2015). The federal government spends less than $28 billion on welfare (Schott, Povetti & Finch, 2012).

Controversies surround arguments for redistribution of wealth, so topics like reparations for slavery, affirmative action, the living wage campaign, and government transfer payments to low-income families as well as to businesses provide excellent topics for debates. Investigating the role of farm subsidies, energy subsidies, and other forms of corporate transfer payments provide an alternate way of looking at how wealth is redistributed in the United States. A debate on the campaign to increase the minimum wage, for instance, gives students the opportunity to compare the needs of businesses to make a profit with the needs of workers to earn a fair wage. Teams can argue how advocates for each side of the issue believe their policies work for the common good.

Social Classes at Your School

Students extend the analysis of class rankings to the social status of groups in their grade at school. While these groups may not be related directly to social class, most schools have popular groups, jock groups, nerd groups, smart groups, and other cluster groups that mirror social class in the wider world. In this activity, students define and map the social groups surrounding them. They list identifiable groups and the categories of students who belong to each group. After defining the groups, they rank them according to the social power each group has. Then they discuss what they believe to be the source of their power.

This is a favorite activity with students. They are well aware of these rankings, but they rarely discuss them openly. This activity brings the dynamics out in the open for analysis. When they analyze social power in school, they begin to question what power really is. Some students define social power as having a few good friends rather than being surrounded by people who may defer to them out of fear.

Social Class and Schooling

The education system reflects class hierarchies and class values. Schooling is largely based on white middle- to upper-class values, and students must acquire the language (grammar, vocabulary, and thought processes) and class aspirations/values (individualistic identity and social mobility) of this particular demographic for success in school. Rothstein's (2004) "Class and the Classroom" discusses how parenting differences among social classes affect school achievement. "Socioeconomic Status and Education" (Andre, Aubry, Battista & Passero, 2008) outlines how local school districts secure funding and how affluent students, as well as socioeconomically disadvantaged students, are affected by the pressures of schooling in America. The website for the American Psychological Association factsheet "Education and Socioeconomic Status" (2015) contains concise information students can digest about the role of social class in education.

Lower classes in society have a tendency toward collective identity and moving into the middle and upper classes of society can be an isolating process. Acquiring an individualistic identity can involve leaving one's collective identity behind, which can engender feelings of betraying one's people. Because teachers often encourage students from lower classes to aspire to higher education, it is important to understand that these emotional complications can make class advancement difficult.

Oral Interviews: Class Mobility

Interviewing adults who have changed social statuses, especially a family member, makes the concept of class mobility meaningful for students. (Lesson 7.4, *Oral Interview on Social Class*, page 180.) Students ask their interviewee about factors that contributed to their class advancement, what personal qualities helped them (drive, talent, perseverance), who helped them (parents, spouse, mentors), and if they received financial assistance (G.I. Bill, college grants or loans, welfare). They find out how the interviewee grew up and what values his or her family had about money and social class. They can also inquire about the difficult aspects of class advancement. Finally, they conclude by asking their interviewees if they have advice to offer young people. Students write up their interviews and share highlights with the class. They can share informally or make short films, podcasts, or other creative presentations.

Collaborative Research: Schooling in Your City

To explore the class demographics of the city they live in, our students read Richard Florida's (2013) article, "Class Divided Cities: Atlanta Edition." Florida's color-coded maps demonstrate social class demographics in urban centers around the United States (Atlanta, Chicago, New York, Miami, Detroit, Washington, D.C., and Los Angeles), so this lesson can be adapted to other cities. The maps provide students with a visual picture of class dynamics in urban centers, particularly as they affect the quality of schools in particular neighborhoods.

As a follow-up collaborative action project, students choose a public school to investigate. They conduct Internet research to gather demographic information about school zones, including income levels, housing costs, and racial makeup. They compare socioeconomic status with test scores by school. They enter the information into a shared Google document, which makes it easy to visually compare data from schools across the city. Suffice it to say, the results make glaringly obvious the connection between socioeconomic status and success in school. They also show the persistence of racial segregation in schools. Materials for conducting this activity can be downloaded from the iChange Collaborative Teacher Resources page (2016) at www.ichange collaborative.com/ichange/Teacher_Resources.html.

Action Projects

Students conclude the unit by conducting action projects on topics related to homelessness, issues of the working poor, media representations of class, the relationship between poverty and crime, healthcare disparities, middle-class guilt, the wealth gap, minimum wage standards, food and nutrition issues, and health issues faced by low-income families. Students have volunteered in soup kitchens and food banks, conducted clothing drives, read to children in women's shelters, and collected supplies for refugee centers. One group raised money from friends and family members to fund a well in Sierra Leone.

Inquiry Into Social Class: Language Arts/English Connections

Social class has a storied history. Its contradictions rest at the very heart of American identity and are widely reflected in the literary cannon. The works of F. Scott Fitzgerald, Edith Wharton, John Steinbeck, Stephen Crane, and Henry James reflect a near obsession with social class issues. British authors, most notably Charles Dickens, Jane Austen, and George Bernard Shaw, also provide rich selections addressing class.

Book selections for middle-school readers include Hinton's *The Outsiders* (1967/2006), Smith's *A Tree Grows in Brooklyn* (1943/2006), Zuzak's *The Book Thief* (2007), Boyne's *The Boy in the Striped Pajamas* (2006), and Lockhart's *We Were Liars* (2014). Max Berry's (2003) satirical view of a dystopian corporatocracy in *Jennifer Government* bears disturbing parallels to current reality.

Works for older readers that address intersecting themes of race, gender, and social class include Ellison's *Invisible Man* (1952/1995), Morrison's *The Bluest Eye* (1970/2007), Baldwin's *Go Tell It on the Mountain* (1951/2013), Naylor's *The Women of Brewster Place* (1983), King's *Truth and Bright Water* (1999), and Alexie's book of short stories, *Blasphemy* (2013). In Patrice Nganang's novel *Dog Days* (2006), the reader sees the turbulent political environment in Cameroon through the eyes of a dog.

Film analysis can help integrate lessons learned about social class through the power of visual storytelling. *Salt of the Earth* (Biberman, 1954) and *Matewan* (Sayles, 1987) dramatize the intersections of gender and race in the context of union organizing. *Imitation of Life* (Stahl, 1934), a groundbreaking film for its time, explores the relationship between two women (one black and one white) during the Great Depression and demonstrates the effects of race on opportunities for social advancement.

Poetry selections include the works of Langston Hughes, Audre Lorde, April Linder, and Gwendolyn Brooks. The poetry of Thomas Hardy, Allen Ginsberg, and Seamus Heaney also address class issues.

Nonfiction books to supplement the curriculum include selections from Newitz and Wray's collection of essays, *White Trash: Race and Class in America* (1996), Ehrenreich's *Nickle and Dimed: On (Not) Getting by in America* (2011), and hooks's *Where We Stand* (2000).

Conclusion

By the end of this unit, students have explored their race, gender, and class identities, related their experience to wider social patterns, and observed similar patterns among race, gender, and social class oppressions. They have learned about the identities of their classmates through dialogues and formed deeper relationships. They have developed thinking, research, writing, and presentation skills. They have analyzed social problems and taken deliberate action to address them. At the end of each year, we ask them how they have changed, and we measure the outcome of our method by their responses. They report that they are more accepting of themselves and others. They are more comfortable talking about sensitive, yet important, subjects related to social justice. They overwhelmingly report that the interactive exercises are by far the most powerful aspect of the course because through them they make deeper connections with their classmates. They tell us the most important things they learned, they learned from each other.

References

Alexie, S. (2013). *Blasphemy*. New York: Grove Press.

Alvarez, L. & Kolker, A. (2001). *People like us: Social class in America* [PBS special]. New York, NY: Center for New American Media Film Library. Retrieved from www.cnam.com/people-like-us/about/order.html.

Anderson, S. (2012, Oct 25). Seeing through the privilege haze. *Teaching Tolerance*. Retrieved from www.tolerance.org/blog/seeing-through-privileged-haze.

Andre, S., Aubry, K., Battista, P., & Passero, D. (2008). Socioeconomic status and education. WikiEdResearch. *Educational Research and News*. Retrieved from http://wikiedresearch.wikidot.com/socioeconomic-status-and-education.

Baldwin, J. (2013). *Go Tell it On the Mountain*. New York: Vintage International. (Original work published 1951).

Ball, S. (2009, Jan). Interview with professor Stephen Ball. *Education Arena*. New York: Routledge and Taylor & Francis. Retrieved from www.educationarena.com/expertInterviews/interviewcategory2/tedp.asp.

Barone, C. (2000). The foundations of class and classism. (Working Paper 2000). Department of Economics, Dickenson College, Carlisle, PA. Retrieved from http://users.dickinson.edu/~barone/ClassFoundations.PDF.

Berry, M. (2003). *Jennifer Government*. New York: Vintage.

Biberman, H. J. (1954). *Salt of the Earth*. Synergy Entertainment.

Bobo, K. (1993, Mar 14). Pride, prejudice and the not so subtle politics of the working class. *Washington Post*. Retrieved from www.cnam.com/people-like-us/resources/essays1.html.

Boyne, J. (2006). *The Boy in the Striped Pajamas*. Oxford: David Fickling Books.

Brownstein, R. (2013, Apr 25). Meet the new middle class: Who they are, what they want, and what they fear. *The Atlantic*. Retrieved from www.theatlantic.com/business/archive/2013/04/meet-the-new-middle-class-who-they-are-what-they-want-and-what-they-fear/275307/.

By the numbers: A look at the gender pay gap. (2014, Sep 18). *American Association of University Women*. Retrieved from www.aauw.org/2014/09/18/gender-pay-gap/.

Casey, T. & Maldonado, L. (2012). Worst off: Single-parent families in the United States: A cross-national comparison of single parenthood in the U. S. and sixteen other high-income countries. *Legal Momentum, the Women's Legal Defense and Education Fund*. New York: Legal Momentum. Retrieved from www.legalmomentum.org/sites/default/files/reports/worst-off-single-parent.pdf.

Chang, M. L. (2010). Fact sheet: Women and wealth in the United States. *Sociologists for Women in Society*. Retrieved from www.socwomen.org/wp-content/uploads/2010/05/fact_2–2010-wealth.pdf.

Cookson, P. & Persell, C. (1986). *Preparing for Power: America's elite boarding schools*. New York: Basic Books.

Cunha, F. & Heckman, J. (2009). Economics and psychology of inequality and human development. (Working Paper 14695). *National Bureau of Economic Research*. Cambridge, MA. Retrieved from www.npc.umich.edu/news/events/early_life_2009/papers/ele_heckman.pdf.

Education and socioeconomic status. (2015). *American Psychological Association*. Retrieved from www.apa.org/pi/ses/resources/publications/factsheet-education.aspx.

Ehrenreich, G. (2011). *Nickel and Dimed: On (not) getting by in America*. London: Piccador.

Ellison, R. (1995). *Invisible Man*. New York: Vintage International. (Original work published 1952).

Fabrikant, G. (2005, Jun 5). Old Nantucket Warily Meets New. *New York Times*. Retrieved from www.nytimes.com/2005/06/05/us/class/old-nantucket-warily-meets-the-new.html.

Florida, R. (2013, Feb 21). Class divided cities: Atlanta edition. *CityLab: The Atlantic*. Retrieved from www.citylab.com/housing/2013/02/class-divided-cities-atlanta-edition/4613/.

Fussell, P. (1992). Class: A touchy subject. *Class: A guide through the American status system*. New York: Touchstone/Simon & Shuster. Retrieved from http://isites.harvard.edu/fs/docs/icb.topic1199093.files/Unit%201%20Readings/fussell1.pdf.

Heckman, J. J. (2008). Schools, skills, and synapses. *Economic Inquiry, 46*(3), 289–324.

Hinton. S. E. (2006). *The Outsiders*. New York: Speak. (Original work published 1967).

hooks, b. (2000). *Where We Stand: Class matters*. New York: Routledge.

iChange Collaborative Teacher Resources page. (2016). www.ichangecollaborative. com/ichange/Teacher_Resources.html.

Jackson, V. (2010). Questioning class. (Unpublished seminar material). *Healing Circles*, Atlanta, GA.

Killerman, S. (2012). 30+ examples of middle to upper class privilege. *It's Pronounced Metrosexual*. Retrieved from http://itspronouncedmetrosexual.com/2012/10/list-of-upperclass-privilege/.

King, T. (1999). *Truth and Bright Water*. New York: Grove Press.

Lanahan, S. (2009). Fragile families and the reproduction of poverty. *The ANNALS of the American Academy of Political and Social, 621*(1), 111–131.

Langston, D. (1995). Tired of Playing Monopoly? In M. Anderson's & P. H. Collins (Eds.), *Race, Class and Gender: An anthology*. Bellmont, CA: Wadsworth.

Lockhart, E. (2014). *We Were Liars*. New York: Delacorte Press.

Mantsio, G. (1995). Media Magic: Making class invisible. In Rothenberg (Ed.), *Race, class and gender in the United States* (3rd ed.). New York: Martins. Retrieved from http://web.stcloudstate.edu/teore/SocialProblems/MediaMagic.pdf.

McLanahan, S. & Percheski, C. (2008). Family structure and the reproduction of inequalities. *Annual Review of Sociology, 34*, 257–276.

Morrison, T. (2007). *The Bluest Eye*. New York: Vintage International. (Original work published 1970).

Naylor, G. (1983). *The Women of Brewster Place*. New York: Penguin Books.

Newitz, A. & Wray, M. (Eds.). (1996). *White Trash: Race and class in America*. New York: Routledge.

Newman, D. M. (2006). Mass media and images of social class. From Ch. 10, *The architecture of stratification: Social class and inequality. Exploring the Architecture of Everyday Life* (6th ed.). Thousand Oaks, CA: Pine Forge Press. Retrieved from http://studysites.sagepub.com/newman6study/resources/massmedia.htm.

Nganang, P. (2006). *Dog Days: An animal chronicle*. (A. B. Reid, Trans.). Charlottesville, VA: University of Virginia Press.

O'Neill, J. H. (1997). *The Golden Ghetto: The psychology of affluence*. Milwaukee, WI: Affluenza Project.

Putnam, R. D. (2015). *Our Kids: The American dream in crisis*. New York: Simon & Schuster. (Kindle version). Retrieved from Amazon.com.

Rothstein, R. (2004, Oct). Class and the classroom. American School Board Journal. Retrieved from http://www2.widener.edu/~spe0001/266Web/266Webreadings/class&edRoth06.doc.

Sayles, J. (1987). *Matewan*. Cinecom Entertainment Group.

Smith, B. (2006). *A Tree Grows in Brooklyn*. New York: Harper Perennial Modern Classics. (Original work published 1943).

Stahl, J. M. (1934). *Imitation of Life*. NBC Universal.

Sullivan, L., Meschede, T., Dietrich, L., & Shapiro, T. (2015). The racial wealth gap: Why policy matters. *Institute for Assets and Social Policy*, Brandeis University.

United States Census Bureau, Poverty: 2014 Highlights. Retrieved from www.census.gov/hhes/www/poverty/about/overview/.

Wealth: Having it all and wanting more. (2015, Jan). *Oxfam issue briefing*. Retrieved from www.oxfam.org/sites/www.oxfam.org/files/file_attachments/ib-wealth-having-all-wanting-more-190115-en.pdf.

Zuzak, M. (2007). *The Book Thief*. New York: Alfred A. Knopf.

7

Inquiry Into Social Class: Sample Lesson Plans and Handouts

Social Class Categories: Labels and Stereotypes

Lesson Objectives

Students will

- critically examine media images;
- gain understanding of the influence of media in self-identification;
- gain understanding of the influence of media to perpetuate stereotypes;
- explore ways to support and change media stereotyping;
- explore how they can act as allies to each other;
- create positive images to counteract negative stereotypes;
- write reflective responses about insights they have gained.

Materials Needed

- Newman (2006), Mass Media and Images of Social Class.
  http://studysites.sagepub.com/newman6study/resources/massmedia.htm
- Mantsio (1995), Media Magic—Making Class Invisible
  http://web.stcloudstatw.edu/teore/SocialProblems/MediaMagic.pdf
- Internet for searching for media images related to social class

Suggested Format

- In small groups, ask students to brainstorm positive and negative associations they have for the following groups: upper class, middle class, and lower class.
- Ask them to compare and contrast the characteristics they have outlined for each group.
- Ask them where their associations come from: family, media, peers, or personal experience.
- After students have read the two articles above, have the groups generate five examples from media (television, film, novels, advertising, or music) that demonstrate how the media portrays social classes.
- Groups can also create collages from media images found on the Internet using a collage-making app such as PicCollage (pic-collage.com).

Questioning Class

Lesson Objectives

Students will

- reflect on their own class identities;
- share personal experiences related to social class and listen to others.

Materials Needed

- "Questioning Class" (student handout)

Suggested Format

- Give students the opportunity to complete the "Questioning Class" handout in class or ask them to complete it for homework.
- In class, ask students to share some answers from their questionnaires. Use the following questions to guide the discussion.

  – How do you feel about the social class you are in? (Embarrassed? Guilty? Inferior? Superior?)
  – What is your neighborhood like? Do people from different social classes live there? Different races?
  – What stereotypes might other people have about your class?
  – What stereotypes do you have about other classes?
  – What values does your family have about money and social class?

Questioning Class

1. How would you describe the socioeconomic status of your family? What class are you in?

2. How is money talked about in your family? Between adults? Between adults and children?

3. How would you describe the socioeconomic status of the community you were raised in? What is your neighborhood like?

4. What messages have you received about people who make more money or come from a higher socioeconomic class than your family?

5. What messages have you received about people who make less money or come from a lower socioeconomic class than your family?

6. How do you think people with less money or who come from a lower socioeconomic class view your family?

7. How do you think people with more money or who come from a higher socioeconomic class view your family?

8. How has your socioeconomic status influenced your perception of your self? Of others?

9. How have issues of socioeconomic status influenced your relationships? (With parents, siblings, friends, significant others, etc.?)

10. List 3–5 values that guide your relationship to money or material wealth (Gaining social status, education, helping others, being independent, saving money, vacation or recreation time, being thrifty, etc.)

Adapted from Vanessa Jackson, *Healing Circles*, Atlanta, GA.

Social Class Statistics Web Quest

Lesson Objectives

Students will

- collaborate to research statistics using Internet sources;
- report their finding to the class;
- discuss their results, listening and sharing respectfully;
- compare sources and variables in statistics.

Materials Needed

- "Social Class Statistics" (student handout)

Suggested Format

- Form seven groups to collaborate on research questions.
- Give each group a series of questions to research.
- After students complete the questions, teams present what they have found to the entire class.
- Guide students to recognize that different sources may contain different data. Emphasize the need to use multiple sources to gain accurate data.
- After each group has reported, ask the students:

  - What have you learned?
  - What do you think now?
  - What do you want to know now?

Social Class Statistics

Team One

1. Average U.S. household income

   Answer: _____

   Source: _____

2. Median U.S. household income

   Answer: _____

   Source: _____

3. Percentage of American households that spend more than 50 percent of their income on housing

   Answer: _____

   Source: _____

4. An additional interesting statistic about income and social class you located

   Answer: _____

   Source: _____

Team Two

1. Average net worth of the top 1 percent of wage earners in the U.S.

    Answer: _____

    Source: _____

2. Average net worth of the bottom 40 percent of wage earners in the U.S.

    Answer: _____

    Source: _____

3. What is the average net worth for upper-, middle-, and lower-class families?

    Answer: _____

    Source: _____

4. An additional interesting statistic about net worth and social class you located

    Answer: _____

    Source: _____

Team Three

1. Definition of "Poverty" in the United States in terms of earnings per year

    Answer: _____

    Source: _____

2. Percentage of children in the United States who live in poverty

    Answer: _____

    Source: _____

3. Among the 17 industrial nations, where does the United States rank in terms of the largest percentage of population in poverty?

    Answer: _____

    Source: _____

4. An additional interesting statistic about poverty you located

    Answer: _____

    Source: _____

Team Four

1. Percentage of U.S. children who live in poverty

   Answer: _____

   Source: _____

2. Percentage of U.S. adults who live in poverty

   Answer: _____

   Source: _____

3. Percentage of single mothers who live in poverty

   Answer: _____

   Source: _____

4. An additional interesting statistic about poverty you located

   Answer: _____

   Source: _____

Team Five

1. Median net worth of white Americans

    Answer: _____

    Source: _____

2. Median net worth of African Americans

    Answer: _____

    Source: _____

3. Median net worth of Hispanics in the United States

    Answer: _____

    Source: _____

4. An additional interesting statistic about race and social class you located

    Answer: _____

    Source: _____

Team Six

1. What is the current minimum wage in the United States?

    Answer: _____

    Source: _____

2. What do you earn per year if you work 40 hours/week for the minimum wage?

    Answer: _____

    Source: _____

3. Percentage of minimum wage workers who have paid sick leave

    Answer: _____

    Source: _____

4. An additional interesting statistic on minimum wage you located

    Answer: _____

    Source: _____

Team Seven

1. Percentage of people who graduate from college by class (upper, middle, lower)

   Answer: _____

   Source: _____

2. Average SAT scores for students from middle-class families

   Answer: _____

   Source: _____

3. Average SAT scores for students from lower-income households

   Answer: _____

   Source: _____

4. An additional interesting statistic on education and social class you located

   Answer: _____

   Source: _____

Possible Websites to Consult

U.S. Census Bureau (www.census.gov)

Moody's Economy.com (www.economy.com)

Urban Institute (www.urban.org)

U.S. Department of Commerce (www.commerce.gov)

Economic Policy Institute (www.epi.org)

Habitat for Humanity (www.habitat.org)

Housing Assistance Council (www.ruralhome.org)

ACLU (www.aclu.org)

Human Development Reports (hdr.undp.org/en/)

United for a Fair Economy (www.faireconomy.org)

Oral Interviews: Social Class

Lesson Objectives

Students will

- practice interview skills in an oral history interview;
- practice listening skills in conducting the interview;
- document the interview;
- prepare a creative presentation;
- share their findings in class.

Materials Needed

- "Oral Interview: Social Class" (student handout)

Suggested Format

- Go over the "Oral Interview: Social Class" handout with students.
- Give students a week to complete their interviews.
- Give students another week to prepare their presentations.
- Have students give their presentations to the class.
- Conclude the project by having students write a one-page response on what they learned from their interviews and from hearing other's presentations.

Oral Interview: Social Class

Instructions

1. Interview an adult, preferably one who has changed social class statuses, about how class status has affected his or her life. You can use the questions below for guidance, but allow the person you are interviewing to share stories that go beyond these questions.

2. Make an audio recording of your interview, if possible. If not, take notes.

3. Prepare a creative presentation on the highlights of your interview to share with the class.

Guiding Questions for Interview

1. When you were growing up, what social class were you a member of?

2. In previous generations, what was your family's social status?

3. What values did your family teach you about money?

4. What values did they teach you about education?

5. Did your socioeconomic status change over the course of your life?

6. If so, what happened? If you advanced, to what do you attribute your success?

7. Did particular people help you advance?

8. Did you have any government assistance? (G. I. Bill, student loans, welfare)

9. What has been the most important value in your life?

10. What advice would you give young people today about money or success?

8

Teacher Identity Work

In a presentation to teachers, Martha asks, "What's great about teaching?" After a brief pause, an elementary teacher on the front row raises her hand. "Seeing the light go on," she says, "You see it on a kid's face." Other teachers nod in agreement. Oman writes her response on a flip chart.

"Relationships with students," calls a voice from the back.

"Learning," says another, "I'm always learning." Again, other teachers nod.

Teachers call out responses from all over the room. The list grows: the pleasure of spending time with children; the gratitude of students (even years later); witnessing growth and achievement; knowing their work makes a difference; developing expertise; working with other teachers who share their values; and, of course, having the summer break to recuperate.

After the group exhausts the rewards of teaching, we shift gears and ask another question: "What's not so great about teaching?" Oman flips to a new page to record their answers.

"Knowing what needs to be done to help a student but not having the resources or the authority to do it," a man calls out, and an audible response of agreement rises from the crowd.

"Amen!" says a woman sitting across the room, "Teaching for the test!"

"Not being able to sleep at night," says a woman, frustration in her voice. "I worry about my kids, but I don't have time to address their real issues, because if I don't get their test scores up, my job is on the line!" The crowd responds, indicating that sleepless nights are not uncommon in a profession in which deep care and low authority are the norms.

As the activity continues, the frustration in the room builds. The list grows to include large class sizes; students whose needs outstrip a teacher's capacity to give; disrespect from students (and sometimes parents); unrealistic demands from administrators (who sometimes have little classroom experience); the enormous demands of assessment; time-consuming paperwork; not enough time to teach; the demands of covering a scope and sequence rather than taking the time to ensure that students are actually learning; focusing on intellectual rigor while students' physical or emotional needs remain unmet; bureaucracy and red tape; top-down curricula design; the lack of respect for teaching in society; No Child Left Behind; Race to the Top; Common Core State Standards; teacher assessment programs designed by people who don't teach; long hours; low pay; exhaustion; and burnout. The energy in the room becomes palpable as teachers mirror each other's concerns.

Teaching is a high art and, for many, a calling. The profession bestows enormous rewards, yet in today's acutely political education climate, teacher identity is at risk. National trends toward privatization, standardized testing, and prescribed professional development training have robbed teachers of authority in their classrooms. The deep concern teachers feel for their students combined with limited authority to act on their behalf results in enormous conflict. Teachers feel their expertise goes unrecognized, not only within the field, but also in society at large. Rather than being rewarded for staying in the classroom and refining their craft over subsequent years, teachers who stay in the classroom are seen as lacking the potential for advancement. "Those who can do, and those who can't, teach," the saying goes.

Breen (2014) calls for education programs to prepare teachers to resist the "justateacher" status relegated to them by the "counter-imposed teacher identities of compliance and normalization," so often enforced by schools (p. 126). She laments that "as a collective profession, teachers lack autonomy and democratic space within which to co-create identity and recognition" (p. 132).

Teachers who integrate their own identities into their teaching models are more effective and happier teachers. Palmer (1998) reminds us that we teach who we are rather than what we know. Agne (1999) describes the transformation of her own identity as a teacher, beginning with the realization that her young students were imitating her attitudes and behaviors. She realized she was modeling identity:

> It would be necessary, therefore, to reflect deeply upon who I was and who, as a result, my students would be learning to become. The first responsibility of a teacher, I surmised, was to work consciously and diligently toward reaching self-actualization, that is, to aspire to become the highest potential me.
>
> (p. 166)

Teachers who fail to explore their own identities, not only in terms of race, gender, class, and religion, but also as teachers, are more likely to reproduce inequities in their classrooms. Tickle (1999) emphasizes the need for teacher educators to:

> . . . foster a revisionist perspective of personally reflexive and socially critical-active teachers . . . capable of bringing about personal, educational, and social change rather than instructional technicians who implement policies devised by others, policies that might result in the continuation of social inequalities, discrimination, injustices and narrow worldviews.
>
> (p. 122)

According to Clark and Flores (2014), forming a strong teacher identity is crucial to effective teaching because a teacher's strong sense of self impacts student achievement positively. They describe a transformational model of teacher identity development in which teachers gain a deeper sense of how their own identities have been socially constructed. In turn, they can better support their students, whose identities are under formation.

> . . . forming a strong teacher identity is crucial to effective teaching because a teacher's strong sense of self impacts student achievement positively.

Teacher Identity Threat

In a teacher workshop, a middle school teacher share a story of meeting a man at a party. When she told him what she did for a living, he said, "Oh, I'm sorry." The group laughed, because they had all faced social situations in which their teaching identities were subtly (or not-so-subtly) diminished. A high school teacher shared a remark his twenty-something nephew made at a family dinner: "I've thought of going into teaching if my current career doesn't work out." Teachers of color, particularly men, reveal an additional layer of identity threat. They are sometimes charged with modeling success for their race by achieving status that brings the entire group up. An African American man shared that his father couldn't understand why he wanted to teach. "Why are you wasting your time? You could be doing so much more."

Teachers tell us they also bear the brunt of so-called "positive" stereotypes, the lauding of teaching as a noble profession. "I could never do that!" they hear. "You must be a saint!" or "How do you stand it? I could never work around little kids," or "Teenagers are so disrespectful. You deserve a medal!" These well-meaning comments subtly position their relationships with students as antagonistic. Lest we forget, students are the very reason they teach in the first place.

Teacher Blaming

Teachers are blamed for persistent social and educational problems they did not create and have no power to solve. Kumashiro (2012) characterizes teaching as:

> . . . not merely a profession that receives little praise. Rather, it has become a profession that is blamed with all that is wrong with education. Students not learning? Then it's because teachers are not smart enough, skilled enough, hard working enough. Gains in student achievement are not sufficient? Create incentives to make teachers work harder, work smarter, and innovate their way to success, all the while regulating and monitoring them. Schools are still failing? Get rid of those teachers.
>
> (p. 45)

Kumashiro associates teacher blaming with the nation's current obsession with high stakes testing, which narrows the curriculum and curtails teachers' authority over what and how they teach. Taubman (2012) suggests that teacher blaming may say more about society's unconscious desires for education to be a vehicle of utopian dream fulfillment than it does about teachers. He argues that our preoccupation with teacher blaming serves to mask more fundamental problems in education. Ladson-Billings (2006) sees what we call the achievement gap, not as the fault of teachers, but rather as a result of our nation's "education debt," pointing to the persistent marginalization of people of color from educational access. She views the current emphasis on raising test scores as a distraction that allows deeper inequities in society and schooling to persist. Ball (2009) calls quantitative assessments of teachers "oppressive" and suggests that the practice runs the risk of producing "drones, technicians who have no sense of sociality, no sense of principled judgment; they just do what they need to do to push up the performance indicators" (pp.6–7). Such measures discourage risk-taking, suppress innovation, and stifle creative agency.

Business as Usual

Education is a $500 billion business funded primarily through tax dollars (Hargreaves & Fullan, 2012; Kumashiro, 2012). The shift toward the business model of education began in the 1980s and continues into the present. Billions of dollars in services and products are outsourced to for-profit companies. The standards-and-testing movement, fueled by the fear of a failing educational system, has created opportunities for large-scale corporations to respond with educational products. High-stakes testing requires test booklets and answer sheets, tutoring services, and study guides. Standardization calls for scripted curricula designed to raise test scores, textbooks, worksheets, teacher guides, and training manuals, all of which must be purchased by schools and districts. Besides the production and sale of standardized materials, school management, particularly in charter schools, is increasingly outsourced to for-profit companies.

Hargreaves and Fullan (2012) contrast the business capital model of education with the professional capital model. In the business capital model, education is seen primarily as a market for business, with huge investment opportunities in technology, curriculum, testing, assessment, training, and school management. Schools themselves are seen as vehicles for profit. In this view, teaching is ideally a low investment enterprise, requiring little education. In a top-down, hierarchical business system, teachers are hardly professionals; they are little more than clerks in a delivery system of pre-programmed instruction.

The development of professional capital, by contrast, requires social vision and long-term investment in human beings from birth to adulthood. In this model, teachers are "highly committed, thoroughly prepared, continuously developed, properly paid, well networked with each other to maximize their own improvement, and able to make effective judgments using all their capabilities and experience" (Hargreaves & Fullan, 2012, p. 3).

Defining only certain teaching methods to be "scientifically proven" privileges certain kinds of knowledge in research and influences funding (Kumashiro, 2012). Research traditionally relies on the fundamental concepts of dominant ideology (associated with white, male, middle class identities) to legitimize knowledge. Delpit (2006) addresses the skepticism with which many people of color approach educational research: "Academic research has, after all, found us genetically inferior, culturally deprived and verbally deficient," she writes (p. 31). She claims such research-based "knowledge" has increased social disparities in education rather than alleviated them.

Academic research also privileges measurable knowledge over the clinical knowledge teachers acquire in the classroom through working with and knowing their students.

Beginning in the 1950s, the United States' government targeted inequalities related to race, gender, disabilities, and income status in schools. In more recent years, programs such as No Child Left Behind and Race to the Top have endorsed market-based solutions. Kumashiro (2012) outlines the ideology that framed this shift: Education should be administered by a centralized, top-down hierarchy that reflects a patriarchal family with the father at the helm. Teachers play the traditionally subservient role of mother, nurturing children, but always answering to a higher authority. They act as clerks whose authority to think and act is strictly limited. They are given scripts to read and scenarios to act out in their classrooms, roles conceived for them by their superiors. They are judged by standards they played no part in creating and which do not necessarily reflect their interests, values, education, or capabilities. Like women in traditional societies, classroom teachers have been conditioned to passively acquiesce to authority, to not make waves. If they give voice to their concerns, they risk being labeled as complainers. Like cogs in a very large machine, they feel powerless to change the current course of top-down management in their profession.

(White) Women's Work

In 2011, 62 percent of public school teachers were white women (Chance & Toldson, 2013). Historically, K-12 education has been white women's work, and consequently, many of the same identity issues that affect the psychology of white women affect the psychology and identity of teachers. In the nineteenth century, young white women were recruited en masse into teaching. True to the gender norms of the time, these women were expected to be subservient to men in their homes and to male administrators in schools. According to Kahn (2014), women were believed to have natural characteristics that made them ideal for teaching: purity, morality, and nurturance. The view of teacher as surrogate mother reinforced the idea that teaching was a "natural" occupation for women, thus feminizing the profession.

For white women, in particular, identity was constructed to render them compliant to authority and subservient to a patriarchal, white supremacist social structure. Kumashiro (2012) connects the expanding of the role of white women in education to the "colonizing, assimilating mission of public schooling in United States," in which schools attempted Pygmalion-style makeovers of native peoples, people of color, the working class, and the poor. Such pedagogies were designed to subordinate and erase non-assimilating cultures' values and perspectives. Two centuries later, too little has changed:

> White women teachers even today symbolize the goal of public schooling to assimilate difference, all couched in the image of nurturing and care, as depicted in popular Hollywood films like *Dangerous Minds* and *Freedom Writers*, where young White women teachers lift up their poor students of color.
>
> (p. 13)

White women were also a source of cheap labor. The low status of the teaching profession is securely tied to it being predominantly female. The feminization of teaching and its association with "women's work" has impacted equality in terms of wages, career advancement, and professional authority. The positions of men and women in the profession mirrors their position in the labor market in general, with female teachers occupying positions in lower grades and male educators disproportionately represented in higher paid positions in secondary schools, higher education, and administration, despite corresponding levels of education in women (Kelleher, 2011). Kahn (2014) writes that "teaching is so closely linked with femininity that men who go into the field often face social repercussions to their masculinity" (p. 116). Breen (2014) concurs: "To be associated with this identity is to be feminized, which is perceived as a socially unacceptable identity for a male" (p. 125). These concerns have resulted in calls for more men to enter the teaching field as a means of raising the professional status of teaching. Another reason for the recruitment of men into teaching concerns the perceived need for male role models to address gaps in achievement outcomes of boys in certain subjects (Kelleher, 2011, p. 22).

Breen (2014) writes: "The creative act of teaching is inextricably linked to the positive identity development of teachers." Teacher identity, dependent on a strong sense of power and agency, however, is complicated in "a gendered profession founded upon patriarchal hierarchies," where teachers are afforded few spaces in which to construct strong identities (p. 123).

The Additional Tax on Teachers of Color

There is a desperate need for more teachers of color in schools. In 2011, 76 percent of public school teachers were white, 9.3 percent were African American, 7.4 percent were Hispanic, 2.3 percent were Asian, and 1.2 percent identified as another race (Kelleher, 2011). Teacher demographics do not match student demographics, and consequently students of color are often taught by white teachers who do not look like them, talk like them, or understand their experience.

This is a particular problem for the self-image of black male students, as black men comprise less than two percent of the teaching force. Toldson (2011) calls for the recruitment of black men into the teaching profession, reminding us that the ratio of white female teachers to white female students is 1 to 15, while the ratio of black male teachers to black male students is 1 to 534. Not withstanding the need to recruit black men into teaching, white women must respond by building strong, dynamic relationships across difference with black male students.

Research shows that teachers of color leave teaching at higher rates than their white counterparts (Borman & Dowling, 2008; Dilworth & Coleman, 2014). As national demographics change, more students of color enter our schools, and yet the growth of teachers of color has shrunk rather than grown to meet the need. Students of color need teachers who can relate to them. They need to know that there *are* teachers who "get" them and have similar family and cultural backgrounds and values. Because there is a dearth of teachers of color in the field, the teachers of color who are there bear a disproportionate burden. Students of color seek them out for relationships. They are the ones who hear the stories of subtle and not-so-subtle discrimination by white teachers; microaggressions from well-meaning white students; and sometimes downright racial slurs and insults. Because white teachers are often unprepared to take responsibility for supporting the racial identities of their students, this responsibility falls to teachers of color. One teacher in our workshop referred to her role as a teacher of color in a predominantly white school as "an extra part time job I don't get paid for." She spent so much time counseling students of color, listening to their stories, validating their feelings, and helping them figure out how to respond to the racism they encountered that she fell behind in other areas of her job. Another teacher shared that he was expected to support white teachers who have

> As national demographics change, more students of color enter our schools, yet the growth of teachers of color has shrunk rather than grown to meet the need.

issues with students of color. White teachers sought him out for advice because they assumed he understood why their students of color sometimes were hard to reach or treated them with disrespect. Negotiating racial misunderstandings between white teachers and students of color becomes an unwritten part of a teacher of color's job description. Teachers of color who resist being cast in this role or who draw boundaries around their time or who bring attention to this dynamic are sometimes seen as uncooperative or labeled "not team players." Teachers who advocate on behalf of students of color risk being accused of "stirring up controversy." African American teachers who advocate for more awareness of racial identity through curricula, professional development, or community programs risk being viewed as having "a black agenda" or "making everything about race." Defensive responses from white teachers indicate they need a deeper understanding of their own racial identity, as well as understanding of the identity formation process for people of color.

Teachers of color are not only expected to support racial identity formation in students of color, but also have to protect themselves from stereotype threat. "I always have to watch myself," says an African American teacher. "I have to be careful not to do anything to reinforce the stereotypes." African American women, in particular, hesitate to voice their concerns about race lest they be stereotyped as "an angry black woman."

Lathan (2014) addresses the crippling fear that many white teachers have about engaging with students of color in authentic ways. She emphasizes the need for white educators to forge connections with students of color as well as their parents and to hold them to high standards. She encourages white educators to let students know how much they care. Greenberg (2015) addresses the complexities that come with whites working for racial justice. "White privilege can lead to a chronic case of undiagnosed entitlement, creating poor listeners, impatient speakers who talk over others, and people unaccustomed to taking orders." Greenberg, nonetheless, believes it is time for whites to adopt a far larger role in educating about race and racism. He provides a list of resources for teachers on his website, Citizenship & Social Justice.

Overcoming Isolation Through Relationships

Teachers often work behind closed doors in the private worlds of their classrooms where they are the only adult present. The issues and conflicts they invariably encounter with students, parents, and administrators may be internalized as personal problems rather than analyzed as social patterns prevalent in an inequitable institutional system. Isolation is a key component of any form of oppression, and teaching, as we know it, is inherently isolating.

> Teachers need to form relationships with other teachers so they can exchange mutual support and gain authority over their work. They need spaces to voice their concerns among peers who share their struggles and appreciate their successes. When this happens, they gain a sense of solidarity that validates their identity and self-worth.

Teachers need to form relationships with other teachers so they can exchange mutual support and gain authority over their work. They need spaces to voice their concerns among peers who share their struggles and appreciate their successes. When this happens, they gain a sense of solidarity that validates their identity and self-worth.

In our teacher workshops, teachers share classroom experiences, conflicts, success stories, and lesson plans. So conditioned are teachers to work in isolation that they sometimes tell us they feel guilty, as if they are "stealing," when they adopt another teacher's method or a lesson plan. Yet teachers are hungry for connections with each other. They consider the relationships they form with each other during our workshops to be a key benefit of our program. Like students, they feel honored to bear witness to each other's stories and often see their own issues reflected in the experiences others share. These nurturing relationships often last for years, as teachers stay in contact through online forums and other professional development experiences.

It's the System, Stupid

We know enough about what works in education to know that teachers are not always the problem. Yet somehow such knowledge is obscured by the politics of education. We know that small class sizes make a difference. We know that when students feel cared for and appreciated by teachers, they achieve more. We know that teachers who form positive relationships with their students are more effective. We know when teachers have more authority over what they teach and the methods they use, their enthusiasm increases, and they feel more empowered professionally and personally. We know that small, dynamic learning communities generate knowledge and inspire learning. We know that teachers gain inspiration from professional relationships with other teachers through collaborating, co-teaching, networking, sharing professional growth opportunities, and participating in teacher support groups.

Teachers are charged with preparing the next generation to be informed citizens, critical thinkers, and creative problem solvers. To meet this challenge, we must form relationships across difference with like-minded colleagues who offer encouragement and support. We need to create spaces for teachers to explore their relationships with power and agency, so they can act with conscious intention in ways that serve their students.

Grace Lee Boggs (2012) calls for much more than reform. She calls for revolution: "We need a paradigm shift in our concept of education. We must view the movement to transform our schools as just as vital to our twenty-first century humanity as the civil rights movement was to our twentieth century humanity" (p. 136). Boggs explains that while rebellion disrupts society, revolution envisions a more advanced human being. The purpose of education can no longer serve to increase individual earning power or to supply workers to industry, says Boggs. "Children need to be given a sense of the unique capacity of human beings to shape and create reality in accordance with conscious purpose and plans" (p. 137). Students need to be given opportunities to solve real-world problems in their communities and make connections between the dialectic interplay of their inner and outer environments. Boggs sees revolution as the struggle to transform relationships:

> Transforming relations means that revolution is not about the oppressed switching places with the oppressors, nor is it about the "have-nots" acquiring the material possessions of the "haves." It is about overcoming the "dehumanization" that has been fostered by the commodification of everything under capitalism and building more democratic, just, and nourishing modes of relating to people".
>
> (p. 148)

Schools can be transformed from institutions designed to teach conformity and complicity, instruments that reproduce inequalities and reproduce social class distinctions, institutions that blame their victims rather than taking responsibility for correcting their own mistakes. Teacher education can move from "training" programs to teacher empowerment programs.

> Schools can become places that affirm the humanity of students.

There is a way out. Put teachers in charge of teaching. Schools can become places that affirm the humanity of students. A new system of transformative learning would define teachers as facilitators of self-directed student learning. Students would be identified as knowledge creators and change makers. The goal of any curriculum would be the accomplishment of personal agency and self-authorship in the context of a dynamic community.

Change is not an option; it is an imperative.

References

Agne, K. J. (1999). Caring: The way of the master teacher. In R. P. Lipka & T. M. Brinthaupt (Eds.), *The Role of Self in Teacher Development* (pp. 165–188). Albany, NY: State University of New York Press.

Ball, S. (2009, Jan). Interview with Professor Stephen Ball. *Education Arena.* Routledge and Taylor & Francis. Retrieved from www.educationarena.com/expertInterviews/interviewcategory2/tedp.asp.

Boggs, G. L. (2012). *The Next American Revolution: Sustainable activism for the twenty-first century.* Berkeley, CA: University of California Press.

Borman, G. D. & Dowling, N. M. (2008). Teacher attrition and retention: A meta-analysis and narrative review of the research. *Review of Educational Research, 78*(3), 367–409.

Breen, M. C. (2014). From As If to What If: Interrogating power, agency, space, and self in the feminized position of teacher. In P. M. Jenlink (Ed.), *Teacher Identity and the Struggle for Recognition: Meeting the challenges of a diverse society* (pp. 123–134). Lanham, MD: Rowman & Littlefield.

Chance, W. L. & Toldson, I. A. (2013). *Black Male Teachers: Diversifying the United States teacher workforce.* Bingley, UK: Emerald Group Publishing.

Clark, E. R. & Flores, B. B. (2014). The Metamorphosis of Teacher Identity: An intersection of ethnic consciousness, self-conceptualization, and belief systems. In P. M. Jenlink (Ed.), *Teacher identity and the Struggle for Recognition: Meeting the challenges of a diverse society* (pp. 3–14). Lanham, MD: Rowman & Littlefield.

Delpit, L. (2006). *Other People's Children.* New York: The New York Press.

Dilworth, M. E. & Coleman, M. J. (2014). *Time for a Change: Diversity in teaching revisited.* Washington, DC: National Education Association.

Greenberg, J. (2015, Jul 10). Curriculum for white Americans to educate themselves on race and racism: From Ferguson to Charleston. *Citizenship and Social Justice.* Retrieved from http://citizenshipandsocialjustice.com/2015/07/10/curriculum-for-white-americans-to-educate-themselves-on-race-and-racism/.

Hargreaves, A. & Fullan, M. (2012). *Professional Capital: Transforming teaching in every school.* New York: Teachers College Press.

Kahn, M. (2014). The Irony of Women Teachers' Beliefs About Gender. In P. M. Jenlink (Ed.), *Teacher Identity and the Struggle for Recognition: Meeting the challenges of a diverse society* (pp. 113–122). Lanham, MD: Rowman & Littlefield.

Kelleher, F. (2011). *Women and the Teaching Profession: Exploring the femininisation debate.* London: United Nations Educational, Scientific and Cultural Organization (UNESCO).

Kumashiro, K. (2012). *Bad Teacher! How blaming teachers distorts the bigger picture.* New York: Teachers College Press.

Ladson-Billings, G. (2006). From the achievement gap to the education debt: Understanding achievement in U. S. schools. *Educational Researcher, 35*(7), 3–12.

Lathan, C. (2014). Dear white teacher. *Rethinking Schools, 29*(1). Retrieved from www.rethinkingschools.org/archive/29_01/29_01_lathan.shtml.

Palmer, P. J. (1998). *The Courage to Teach.* San Francisco, CA: Jossey-Bass.

Taubman, P. M. (2012). *Disavowed Knowledge: Pyschoanalysis, education and teaching.* New York: Routledge.

Tickle, L. (1999). Teacher Self-Appraisal and Appraisal of Self. In R. P. Lipka & T. M. Brinthaupt (Eds.), *The Role of Self in Teacher Development* (pp. 121–141). Albany, NY: State University of New York Press.

Toldson, I. (2011). White women are 63 percent of the teaching force. Can they teach black boys? Excerpt from: Men in the classroom. *Living Education eMagazine.* Retrieved from www.youtube.com/watch?v=VYo9i1HccpI.